THE BROKER'S MANUAL

VOL 1: LEASING

Thomas Bergman
Michael Bergman
Laurence Bergman

The Broker's Manual Vol. One: Leasing © Published 2018
IZEA HOLDINGS, LLC All rights reserved.

Table of Contents

ABOUT THE AUTHORS 5
FOREWORD 7
FIRST THINGS FIRST 10
INTRODUCTORY REMARKS 11
COMMON SENSE 13
MENTORING 16
    MENTORING CHECKLIST 17
SECTION I: GENERAL OVERVIEW 20
    THE PARTICIPANTS 21
        Lineup for the Tenant 22
        Lineup for the Landlord 23
    TYPES OF LEASES 24
        Office Lease 24
        Industrial Lease 25
        Retail Lease 26
        Ground Lease 27
        Perspective 28
    DEFINITIONS 29
    EXECUTIVE LEASE SUMMARY 44
        Lease Summary Form 45
    COMMERCIAL LEASE CONTACT LIST 48
        Commercial Lease Contact List Form 49
    COMPETITIVE ADVANTAGES 52
        Competitive Advantages Form 53
        Competitive Advantages Form (With Numbers) 57
    NEGOTIATION SKILLS 61

SECTION II: REPRESENTING THE LANDLORD 63
    INTRODUCTION TO REPRESENTING THE LANDLORD 64
    INTERVIEW AND QUALIFICATION OF A PROSPECTIVE LESSEE 68
    PROSPECTIVE TENANT SUMMARY 69
    LISTING AGREEMENTS 72
        Form 1 74
        Form 2 79
    MARKETING MANAGEMENT 88
        General Ideas 88
    Leasing Management Plan 90
    INTRODUCTION TO PRE-LEASE REIMBURSEMENT LETTER AGREEMENT 92
        Pre-Lease Reimbursement Letter Agreement 93
    INTRODUCTION TO LEASE NEGOTIATIONS 95
        Lease Proposal Form 97
        Letter of Intent 100

SECTION III: REPRESENTING THE TENANT 104
    INTRODUCTION TO REPRESENTING THE TENANT 105
    INTRODUCTION TO THE DUE DILIGENCE CHECKLIST 108
        Due Diligence Checklist 109
    INTRODUCTION TO TENANT QUALIFICATION 114
        Tenant Representation Qualification Form 115
    TENANT REPRESENTATION TRANSACTION MODEL 118
    TENANT REPRESENTATIVE LETTER OF ENGAGEMENT AND
REPRESENTATION 120
    RFP 124
    AREA ANALYSIS SCORING 132
    SMART ASKS 134

SECTION IV: ADDITIONAL FORMS 169
    CERTIFICATE OF SUBSTANTIAL COMPLETION 170
        Certificate of Substantial Completion Form 171
        Commencement Date Notice/Memorandum 172
    CALCULATION OF TOTAL COSTS OF OCCUPANCY 174
        Calculation of Total Costs of Occupancy Table 175
    LEASE CHECKLIST 177
    SUPPLEMENTS TO THE LEASING CHECKLIST 197
        Office Supplement 197
        Retail Supplement 198
        Ground Lease Supplement 199
        Industrial Supplement 200

SECTION V: TECHNOLOGY AND MARKETING/PROFESSIONAL RESOURCES
....201
    INTRODUCTION 202

SECTION VI: LEARNING THROUGH EXPERIENCE 208
    INTRODUCTION 209

ABOUT THE AUTHORS

Thomas Bergman has practiced law for 40 years. A graduate of the University of Pennsylvania and University of Cincinnati College of Law, he is principal of Thomas H. Bergman & Assoc., LLC., a boutique law firm providing services to a wide range of clients, many involved in commercial real estate. Licensed as a Title Agent in Ohio and accomplished in sophisticated real estate transactions, he has authored the article titled "Negotiating the Commercial Loan Commitment," which appeared in *The Practical Real Estate Lawyer* and has taught Real Estate Transactions at the University Of Cincinnati College Of Law. Tom has also lectured and served as a guest speaker for continuing legal education programs. Presentations include "How to Structure Worry-Free Commercial Leases." Admitted to the Ohio Bar, the Federal District Court for the Southern District of Ohio, and the U.S. Supreme Court, Mr. Bergman successfully argued the case of *McMillan v. Brune-Harpenau-Torbeck Builders, Inc.* in the Ohio Supreme Court. That case held for the first time in Ohio that privity of contract is not a necessary element of a cause of action against a home builder.

Michael Bergman, an attorney by training, and admitted to practice in Arizona, has been involved in commercial real estate for over a decade in both Georgia and Ohio. A graduate of Washington University in St. Louis and Emory School of Law, Michael has represented national shopping center owners, international retailers, and office clients and has successfully completed numerous complex leasing transactions acting as an agent for both landlords and tenants. He has been appointed receiver for several major properties and this experience has sharpened his focus on the needs of landlords and tenants. A seasoned author, this is Michael's third book. Previously he wrote *Getting to the Quad* and *The Graduate Survival Guide*. Michael is also a co-author on the highly successful *Barron's AP US History Flashcards* – now in its third edition.

Laurence Bergman, a founding member of NAI Bergman, is a licensed real estate broker in Ohio, Kentucky, and Georgia. Larry is a prolific award winner in Commercial Real Estate. In 2014, he was selected to the Midwest Real Estate News Commercial Real Estate Hall of Fame. He was also awarded NAI Global's President's Award – Eastern US Markets. Out of 400 NAI Global affiliates, NAI Bergman was nominated for Company of the Year and recipient of The Eagle Award – Major Markets – US. Larry has been consistently recognized as a Top 10 Costar Power Broker in Sales and/or Leasing transactions and was also recognized by the Cincinnati Business Courier as a Top 10 Commercial Real Estate broker. Through Larry's community efforts, NAI Bergman was selected as the 2012 Blue Ash, Ohio Business Advocate of the Year. Larry has a Bachelor of Science degree in Real Estate, Urban Development and Marketing from Syracuse University. He writes from personal experience in the leasing area. Larry is a principal in a real estate development and investment business, has served as Chairman of the Greater Cincinnati Commercial Real Estate Council, and continues to sit on its board of directors. He has also served on the Lands Commission in the U.S. Federal Court.

FOREWORD

I started working in commercial real estate about 20 years ago. Coming from a completely different profession, it was a major career transition for me. I had much to learn. After two intense weeks in my new profession, it was time to blow off some steam at a Saturday night party.

A friend approached me and asked if I was enjoying the new job. I assured him that I was, and then he asked me a question: "Now that you're in real estate, you'll know this – What are the stores that are going into the shopping under construction along the West Dodge Expressway?"

I had no idea. I remembered thinking I should know things like that and told him I would find out. Later during the party, two other friends asked me real estate-related questions, one about a new office building and another about the increase in condos available for sale downtown. I didn't know how to answer those questions either.

After returning home late that night, I started thinking about those three questions. I had spent my first two weeks in commercial real estate trying to learn about listing agreements, load factors and how to negotiate a triple-net lease. Nobody at the party asked about those things. Nobody there cared about purchase agreements and lease analyses. Instead, they wanted to know about the sexy parts of my new profession such as prestigious retailers, fancy office buildings and high-priced condos. A revelation suddenly hit me like a ton of bricks. I had joined a fascinating industry! Outsiders saw my job as glamorous.

Everyone, and I mean EVERYONE, is interested in commercial real estate. Over the past 20 years I have fielded similar real estate-related questions more times than I can count.

Indeed, commercial real estate is an alluring profession. We deal with landmark skyscrapers, glitzy retailers and sprawling industrial buildings. When talking about money, we throw around big numbers in the millions. The deals we broker create jobs and generate economic activity. Sometimes our work leads to big-time real estate developments that redefine communities.

Not only do commercial real estate brokers engage in fascinating work, their lifestyles are desirable too. In real estate brokerage, you set your own schedule and you essentially work as your own boss. There is no ceiling to your income. Commercial real estate is the ultimate example of the old saying, "the grass is greener on the other side of the fence." As a broker, many of your friends envy you.

But not everything about commercial real estate is rosy. Sometimes the hours are long, the stress can be overwhelming and much of the work is actually tedious. Deals can fall through at the last minute even though you've psychologically "spent the commission check." The glory of brokering a monster deal can quickly be replaced with the agony of legal trouble or your license being placed on probation by the real estate commission.

Commercial real estate is ripe with opportunity, but it's also fraught with peril. That is why you need this book.

Whether you are new to the profession, or a seasoned broker looking to "sharpen your saw," this highly pragmatic handbook will give you a strong grasp of real estate language and best practices. It even provides actual forms and templates you can use immediately to improve your practice.

In real estate and every other profession, lifelong learning and professional development are of the utmost importance. Things change fast, so we can never stop learning and discovering. We should constantly search for that part of our profession we do not yet know, because holes in your knowledge tend to be what lands brokers in court rooms.

The three authors possess many combined decades of real estate experience. Two of them are lawyers, which gives the book a rich legal foundation and provides readers with ideas that will maximize their working relationship with attorneys.

Brokers should never underestimate the importance of their work. They are a critical part of the real estate deal-making process and often end up having a huge impact on their clients' bottom lines. As licensed and hopefully highly compensated professionals, brokers need to be 100-percent committed to diligent, accurate and client-focused work. The Broker's Manual will help you do just that.

This book provides practical, action-oriented content that is designed to help you roll up your sleeves and jumpstart your brokerage practice. But that's not all; throughout the book, the authors do an outstanding job of focusing on ethics. In order to meet your fiduciary obligations as a broker and provide the service your clients deserve, you must be ever professional. There is no substitute for doing things the right way and treating others with respect and decency.

– Jeff Beals

Jeff Beals is an international award-winning author, acclaimed speaker and successful sales consultant. His books include Self Marketing Power: Branding Yourself as a Business of One and Selling Saturdays: Blue Chip Sales Tips from College Football. Visit Jeff Beal's website at jeffbeals.com

FIRST THINGS FIRST

"Ethics is knowing the difference between what you have the right to do and what is right to do."
~ Potter Stewart, United States Supreme Court Justice

A real estate Broker[1] is a licensed practitioner in a profession regulated by the government. We cannot start any volume written for the benefit of the Broker without stressing the importance of vigilant adherence to the laws and rules which govern this business. It is essential for you to comply with regulations and to diligently adhere to applicable codes of ethics and conduct. And don't stop there. Remember to always strive to do the right thing. You are in this business for the long haul; your reputation is paramount.

It is especially important for a person practicing in the field of commercial real estate to understand the rules and laws of Agency and to work to build a foundation for each transaction which assures that the client/customer understands the Agency role of the licensed broker/agent. This book does not discuss Agency Disclosure as each state has its own laws and procedures. It's essential that you understand the laws regarding Agency in the state(s) where you practice. Equally important is your need to clearly communicate your role in a transaction, as required by law.

If you are not sure of the answer to a question regarding compliance, do not hesitate to reach out to your supervisor or counsel. Don't charge ahead – take the opportunity to get the proper guidance.

---

[1] We have elected to use the general term "Broker" throughout the book to cover both the agent and Broker. This is more consistent with the practices in the marketplace.

INTRODUCTORY REMARKS

"In the long history of humankind (and animalkind, too), those who learned to collaborate and improvise most effectively have prevailed."

~ Charles Darwin, *The Origin of Species*

The purpose of this volume is straightforward. A Broker is an essential component in most commercial leases. Often the driver of the lease, the Broker's contribution can significantly impact a client's business for many years. Landlords historically own the turf – they control the property and usually the lease form. But financial and market leverage make nearly every lease an opportunity for meaningful negotiation. The savvy Broker, whether representing the landlord or the tenant, is a valuable resource for the client. The following has been developed in order to explain and highlight practical issues, provide insights, and supplement existing information.

This work is certainly not meant to be exhaustive. Rather it has been developed to be an easy-to-use resource. It is aimed to be practical rather than philosophical. It contains a mixture of advice, background, forms, and procedures. It is very much action-oriented. Undoubtedly in your training to become a licensed agent or broker and in your continuing education courses you have been counseled and cautioned that you are not to practice law. We will state it here and later: be sure to avoid any unauthorized practice of law and whenever you have a question.

While we have provided a number of forms in this text PLEASE BE AWARE OF THE NEED TO INVOLVE YOUR MANAGER AS TO INTERNAL FORMS AND COUNSEL AS TO ANYTHING THAT WILL BE GIVEN TO CLIENTS OR OTHERS. EVEN PROVIDING A CLIENT A FORM CAN BE CONSTRUED AS PRACTICE OF LAW. MAKE SURE YOU ARE UP TO DATE ON YOUR LOCAL REGULATIONS AND REQUIREMENTS.

There are already many opportunities for commercial Brokers to pick up valuable information, but the available resources are often limited in scope or are aimed at all aspects of brokerage – not just commercial leasing. There really are not that many good one-stop specific and practical resources, so we created this manual to fill that void.

Finally, you will notice that we have scattered some purely pragmatic tips throughout the book. These are not necessarily restricted to the practice of leasing but we hope they help you develop rewarding, professional habits. One of the fascinating things about top notch Brokers is the wide-range of personalities and approaches. At a gathering of top performers you will find extroverts and introverts, students of the trade, and folks who tend to be less detail-oriented. But many will share certain characteristics, skills and traits. We have tried to focus on these more universal qualities.

COMMON SENSE

Here is a list of practices and procedures to foster a good relationship with lawyers and clients involved in a leasing deal:

- **Communicate**

    Keep your client and counsel informed. Let the attorney know of business deal developments and changes promptly. Lawyers do not appreciate drafting complex provisions only to be told, "We decided not to do that a long time ago."

- **Play Fair**

    Don't make unreasonable or unfair requests. Try not to set deadlines which ignore the lawyer's schedule. Have the courtesy to set up a meeting or call at a mutually appropriate time. Try to make the lawyer your ally, not your scapegoat.

- **Read**

    Clients and attorneys generally appreciate Brokers who read documents and provide meaningful insight. If you find the lawyer made an error, be helpful and get his/her attention offline – rather than copy a boatload of folks with an emailed "gotcha." But by no means should you ever seek to practice law or play lawyer. DO NOT ENGAGE IN THE UNAUTHORIZED PRACTICE OF LAW. If you have any doubt, consult your counsel or clear your activities with the attorney involved and your direct supervisor.

- **Recognize a Common Goal**

    Seek to accomplish the transaction, but remember that the attorney has a duty to protect the client from risks and is charged with avoiding bad terms and bad deals. You certainly want a commission, but never at the expense of your client by forcing a square peg into a round hole.

- **Know Your Limits**

    You do not – indeed should not – do everything. Know the ethical and legal limits of your assignment and know your own limitations.

- **Be Creative**

    Often you will know the players and the site better than anyone else. If you can craft a solution to a problem, then by all means make a suggestion. For example, a landlord and tenant were caught up in a debate over responsibility for HVAC repairs. The Broker suggested a solution that shifted the repair obligations to the tenant, but only if/after the landlord installed new equipment. This effectively gave an incentive for the landlord to upgrade the space and then reduced its future obligations to maintain.

- **Refer and Choose Wisely**

    Sometimes you may be asked by a client for a lawyer referral. Cultivate lawyers who are experienced and have the right skills and personality to deal with the situation at hand. If the particular transaction requires plenty of sophistication and experience, then recruit an attorney who does sophisticated leasing work. Similarly if your client is leasing a small office for a short term, the choice of counsel may be appropriately adjusted. You can build your own practice by building a go-to stable of attorneys who do excellent work. They will likely reciprocate and will feel comfortable referring work to you if you develop a good relationship and do quality work.

- **Assist**

    If the client (or even the attorney) is not experienced in leasing, you need to assist in educating that person. Help by giving examples and exposing risky positions. Communicate and be patient. Don't make people feel badly because this isn't their field. Try to get this type of client to use an experienced attorney who can serve to protect interests and avoid mistakes, and try to educate the inexperienced lawyer without condescension.

- **Keep Learning**

    A top Broker, one who will be respected within the industry as well as by attorneys, is someone who continuously builds his skills and stays informed on the latest information. What will the new FASB standards do to the market? How will Blockchain impact the entire leasing process over the coming year? Think about other products, learning about the latest issues. Be a leader, not a follower.

- **Work Well with Attorneys**

    We want to stress the need for a good working relationship between the Broker and the attorney. One area that many inexperienced Brokers find difficult is the interface with lawyers. Another is the urge to give legal advice. First of all, lawyers should be viewed as allies, not as adversaries. Moreover, DO NOT PRACTICE LAW UNLESS YOU ARE LICENSED TO PRACTICE LAW. Unfortunately, lawyers sometimes perceive Brokers as being lazy. Sometimes it's a generalization based on a bad experience. More often, however, it's a grossly unfair stereotype. Act in a professional, and caring, and cooperative manner that will reflect well on you and your field. Do what is necessary to make the transaction successful for your client and the good lawyer will appreciate you as a fellow professional.

As mentioned, this volume is organized with an eye to the practical. It is set up in sections after this introductory information. In Section I, we provide a general overview which touches on important concepts and provides certain definitions, plus an overview of common issues you are likely to face whether you represent the landlord or the tenant. In Section II, we provide tools and resources for the Landlord Representative. Section III focuses on the Tenant Representative. In Section IV, we offer more sample forms to serve as templates and idea generators rather than definitive required documents. These hopefully will cut time and save money. After that, in Section V we include some of the technological and industry innovators that can accelerate your practice. Finally, in Section VI we present the wit and wisdom of some top-notch professionals who add their insights, knowledge, and perspective.

MENTORING

Before we jump into Section I of this volume, we would like to take a moment to discuss and explore the value of mentoring. We are strong supporters of the proposition that mentoring is one of the best ways to propel a new Broker into a successful career. All of us have been mentored to some degree and all of us now act as mentors to others. The opportunity to pass on knowledge and experience to others is a gift. It is personally rewarding for the mentor and the mentee, and often yields by economic returns as inexperience turns into skills.

Many companies have well-established mentoring programs. Any beginning Broker should consider himself or herself fortunate to be in that situation. If, however, your situation does not allow you that benefit, think of actively pursuing a mentor. This can be a more senior person in your field or even a fellow Broker in practice who is willing to teach some skills to a new member of the profession. Look into local organizations to see if they can set you up with a mentor.

Attached is a checklist that we have put together which you may find helpful in working with a mentor. It is two-sided and addresses obligations of both parties. After all, this is a symbiotic relationship; therefore, both the mentee and mentor can gain from the experiences.

MENTORING CHECKLIST

I. WHAT IS THE GOAL OF THE MENTORING PROCESS?

   For the Mentee:

   1. Chance to learn from a good role model;
   2. Obtain a sounding board for questions – even the dumb ones;
   3. Receive good advice and feedback when mistakes are made;
   4. Build a network;
   5. Cut the time to assimilate into the industry;
   6. Face challenges so that potential in a mentee turns into results.

   For the Mentor:

   1. Opportunity to pass on learning to a new person;
   2. Expand one's network to a new generation;
   3. Test one's knowledge and expertise against fresh ideas;
   4. Place mentor's career in perspective;
   5. Recharge one's batteries;
   6. Pay back the community.

II. INITIAL MEETING

   For the Mentee:

   1. Before your first meeting, make sure that mentor has been given your resume and contact information.
   2. Tell mentor everything appropriate about where you come from and your background.
   3. Learn what mentor has to say about her/his career and personal background.
   4. Discuss your goals in detail and set up a metric to measure the way you meet the goals through the mentoring relationship.

5. Discuss possible need of adding additional mentors (for example, to explore a specialty).
6. Outline your expectations in terms of availability and time.
7. Schedule future meetings with mentor in terms of frequency, length, and place to meet.
8. Schedule your next meeting.

For the Mentor:

1. Review your background -- how you got here;
2. Ask mentee to tell you about her/himself and her/his career;
3. Outline and discuss your goals;
4. Set out your expectations in terms of time and availability;
5. Set up a schedule of meetings including frequency, length, and place to meet;
6. Schedule your next meeting.

III. AFTER FIRST MEETING

For the Mentee:

1. Go over previous submittals.
2. Go over the progress made on goals.
3. Raise open questions you have that need answers.
4. Consider any other people to consult.
5. Discuss networking opportunities.
6. Assess your progress.
7. Schedule your next meeting.

For the Mentor:

1. Review the materials from last meeting.
2. Discuss progress on goals
3. Discuss areas of progress.
4. Discuss problem areas and strategies for solving issues.
5. Schedule next meeting.

IV. AT THE "END" OF MENTORSHIP[1]

For the Mentee:

1. Summarize the progress and accomplishments in a short, written summary jointly prepared with mentor.
2. Prepare a separate evaluation form from your sole perspective on the program and to process what could be improved/changed.

For the Mentor:

1. Summarize the progress and accomplishments in a short, written summary jointly prepared with mentee.
2. Prepare a separate evaluation form from your sole perspective on the program and to process what could be improved/changed.

---

[1] This suggests termination of the mentorship process. We provide this step to assist with development or a formal program. However, mentorship in the best and most valuable sense is a long – even lifelong – process.

SECTION I: GENERAL OVERVIEW

"Supposing is good, but finding out is better."

~ Mark Twain in Eruption; Mark Twain's Autobiography

THE PARTICIPANTS

To get the lease to the finish line takes more than just a Landlord and a Tenant. The Landlord team and the Tenant team may be somewhat different. The list of participants we are providing will likely be customized to each situation as it arises. For example, in some cases you will need a leasing lawyer and a zoning lawyer. In any event, the quality of your team is very important and you may wish to create a go-to "dream team" for deals with the appropriate contact information for the members all in one place.

In building your dream team, take advantage of the advice of colleagues. Also, build the list through networking and continuing education, and the team itself can often provide its own answers. There are plenty of lawyers who can get you to great environmental consultants, accountants, etc. Make the good experiences known to your co-workers. And, if you have a bad experience let your associates know that too.

While we strongly advocate using a collaborative approach and a multidisciplinary team, take care that there is a clear understanding of responsibilities and accountability. Work with the client to establish who takes the lead and make sure there is good communication within the group.

Lineup for the Tenant

PARTICIPANT	ROLE	APPLICABLE (Y/N)
Tenant	Party seeking new space.	
Tenant Rep Broker	Represents tenant in identifying site and negotiating business terms. May generate RFP and/or letter of intent and help finalize issues. Can be deeply involved in lease process through execution.	
Attorney	Sometimes involved in letter of intent. Reviews lease. Can serve as lease negotiator.	
Architect	Evaluates space; prepares space plan for build out; may be involved in measurement of premises. Can coordinate construction with other consultants.	
Space Planner	Often has similar background/role as architect. Brings expertise to work flow and design. Can save significant money in designing space efficiently.	
Engineer	Inspects premises. Evaluates issues depending on expertise (mechanical/environmental/etc.)	
Insurance Agent	Checks insurance provisions. Provides coverage.	
Accountant	Addresses financial and tax issues for tenant.	
Contractor /Construction Manager	Carries out or oversees the construction; Estimates buildouts.	
Lender	Seeks to protect its security interest. May be concerned about landlord liens. Often wants assurance as to right to remove personal property used as collateral and seeks landlord consent.	
Franchisor (if franchise)	May require specific provisions in order to control franchisee/protect franchisor's rights.	
Title Agent	Can be called upon to check title/issue commitment or policy or title insurance.	
Relocation Specialist	Can help solve packing, moving, and set up/ installation issues.	

Lineup for the Landlord

PARTICIPANT	ROLE	APPLICABLE (Y/N)
Landlord	Owner interested in leasing space. Can be deeply involved or may leave negotiations to property manager, broker, or counsel.	
Broker	Marketing and assistance in negotiation. Advice on pricing and details. Helps get lease completed.	
Attorney	Lease preparation. Often involved in negotiation.	
Lender (if any mortgage)	Possibly has approval rights concerning lease.	
Architect	Designs of building amenities, etc. May be involved in review of work and possibly involved in measurement of space.	
Property Manager	Coordinates showings. Administers lease during term. Provides operating information. May negotiate the terms of the lease.	
Contractor/CM	Build-out if landlord is responsible or review of work if tenant does the build-out.	
Engineer	Depending on the situation various engineers (Environmental/Civil/Mechanical) can play a role in the process.	
Insurance Agent	Provide coverage; coordinate requirements with attorney. Sometimes work with lender.	
Accountant	May assist with tax planning aspects of lease and with evaluation of financial wherewithal of tenant.	
Lease Administrator	In larger organizations, may assist with preparation of forms, circulation of documents, etc.	
Relocation Specialist	May be offered to tenant in lieu of moving allowance or to reduce the amount set aside.	

TYPES OF LEASES

You will typically see four main categories of commercial leases: office, retail, industrial and ground. (Remember – while apartment specialists can be major contributors in brokerage firms, this volume concentrates on the lease. Apartment leases are residential in nature.) These four types of leases are the most common; and often Brokers specialize. You will run into some professionals who simply do "big box" or ones who just work on office leases in large downtown high-rises. These specialists can display deep knowledge in their chosen area. They often know the lease issues intimately – what to ask for and what will fly. But even if you are one of these specialists, some familiarity with lease terms likely to appear in other categories can be very helpful. For example, warehouse leases sometimes include office space areas beyond the distribution or logistics tenant's needs. That space may be cut up and leased to office users. The issues in play in those negotiations may be different than standard industrial lease scenarios.

Included as one of the working tools in Section IV is a Lease Checklist. It will help, but naturally must be adjusted to the special situation. And it is here, in the grey areas, when the extra effort of the quality Broker can shine through. He or she can do this by listening to the client and understanding the site, the lease, and the unique issues of the particular deal.

Office Lease

The office lease category encompasses the many situations where premises are used for general office use. But there are still many variations, exceptions and details. If, for example, the space is let to a medical office, an ancillary laboratory can drag in "industrial" and "retail" issues. The office lease category ranges from corporate and professional office in a downtown setting to a suburban business park. It can be the top floor of a skyscraper or the basement of a laundromat. Naturally, the Broker must be sensitive to the nature of the tenant's business. For example:

- Will the tenant need much parking?

- Are noise issues a big problem? Consider the law office with its need for quiet and confidentiality. Should there be additional soundproofing?

- Will the developer provide exceptional amenities?

- Is there a health club? Common boardroom?

The point of the office lease is to effectively provide a central working place for what may be a long period for a business and its management. The Broker must endeavor to make sure that the common issues of an office lease are considered along with the special issues of the particular building, location and business. Indeed, the little details have a great effect on the economic and enjoyment of the particular lease. For example, by remembering that the head honcho of a prospective tenant has a gigantic ego and insists that he gets an assigned parking spot with his name on it, the Broker can win a big one for the ultimate decision-maker of tenant without significant cost to landlord. Office leases present opportunities to address small items which make big impressions.

Finally, a special form of office lease involves the emerging trend of co-working spaces and social clubs. While typically labeled a "millennial" product, this is such a potent, fast-growing product that nearly all Brokers need to understand how it works.

Industrial Lease

In some way, industrial leases are likely to be slightly less variable than retail or office leases. They are generally less concerned with creature comforts and public impression and tend to center on the efficient storage, movement, or creation of goods. Naturally this is a gross simplification, but industrial Brokers will be generally more concerned with space configuration and dock doors than exclusive use or janitorial details.

Because warehouses or manufacturing facilities are generally large in size, the economic impact of operating expenses is of special interest. Since the type of expense will vary so much between a single-user situation and multi-tenant facilities, there will be different needs depending on the size of the space needed and the market for space. The tenant also may be focused more on a number than quality.

Example: Broker seeks 90,000 square feet for a user within a certain large business park. There are five buildings that fit the bill: one is 120,000 square feet, single-user; one is 200,000 square feet, single-tenant; and three are multi-tenant facilities that can be demised to precisely fit the space need. But the cheapest is old and on two floors, and the most expensive has super-flat floors and extra parking. What is important? Like an office specialist, a good industrial Broker will know much more than the basics. Some supplements for industrial (and all other leases) follow the checklist in Section IV.

Retail Lease

The retail lease can involve extremely high rents - think Fifth Avenue – but it can also include the big box retailer, the class D shopping center spots for the nail shop, and the hip re-use of an eyesore.

When the experienced Broker does retail, he or she will want to be conversant in the goods and merchandise of the particular merchant. Is every store the same? Will the square footage be sufficient to allow the tenant to expand if necessary? Will there be sufficient parking? Parking can be crucial. Retail will need to cover many special areas. This can include exclusive use, subleasing and assignment, hours of operation, continuous use, etc. Think about maintaining a file of solutions to common problems as you complete deals so that you can be a problem solver.

Example: The tenant's standard exclusive use clause bars the landlord from leasing any part of the shopping center to a sporting goods store. But it is a big center and the landlord will not be moved from a stonewall that "this is a non-starter – too broad." You can help alleviate the problem by finding out what sales really bother the prospect. If the tenant sells golf equipment only, should a workout clothing store that sells yoga mats be a problem? Bring some good sense to the situation.

Also, because of the challenges faced by modernized retail in the marketplace, particularly those areas from Internet sales, retail tenants need to be very creative and retail landlords very cautious. Good Brokers will study techniques to service online pickup, drive activity, and reduce costs.

Ground Lease

Ground leases are much less common; however, they can be much more complex than standard space leases. As a result of their rarity and because they can swing huge amounts of money, Brokers can feel lost when facing a ground lease. Remember each side has a lot to lose if the other does not keep its bargain.

Picture the situation: A family trust will never sell its large tract of land which was previously the family farm. But the site is teed-up for a first class office building site, especially since a major hospital has just built a state of the art facility across the street. The landlord knows that if the tenant starts to build a facility and either fails to finish or performs poorly, the landlord will have a property which may be less valuable than the original unimproved tract. These problems need major money to solve. The tenant must get all sorts of answers for the landlord that will allow the tenant to obtain the mortgage it will need and permit the possession of the site for a very long time. The Broker must be able to work with experienced counsel who know the ins and outs of ground lease deals.

Perspective

It bears repeating: keep in mind who you represent. Not only do leases vary in type, but clients do as well. If you represent a tenant, your goals should be aligned with the tenant's goals. Similarly, if you represent the owner, you would have the same goals as the landlord. Do as much homework as you can on the market and the players. If you know that a particular franchise wants to grow in a particular area, or a landlord is in default at other locations, you can use this information to craft appropriate deal provisions. Not only should you try to always be closing, you need to also try to always be learning

DEFINITIONS

- **Accordion Provision**: Clause sometimes found in an industrial lease that allows the tenant to expand/contract its space as conditions warrant.

- **Additional Rent**: Generally means all amounts due under the lease other than the Base Rent. The most common forms of Additional Rent are Operating Expenses, real estate tax and insurance reimbursements, but it can also include late charges, utilities and the like.

- **Advisory Notice**: A notice from landlord informing tenant that the term is about to end and advising that a renewal option needs to be triggered. This is a mechanism to protect the tenant from missing a lease renewal.

- **Anchor Tenant**: A prime tenant in a shopping mall, office building or other project. An Anchor Tenant can attract customers and act as a magnet to bring in other lessees. It is one of the primary reasons that people come to the site and can be a key to the financial viability of the location.

- **AS IS**: The present, existing condition of the premises at the time of lease execution. This includes physical defects and current issues at that time. The aim is to disclaim implied warranties.

- **Assignment**: The transfer by tenant of its interest in a lease. This is different from a Sublease where the subtenant acquires a partial interest. (NOTE: The transfer by a landlord of its rights is also called an Assignment).

- **Attornment**: Tenant's agreement to recognize the lender as a permitted successor to landlord in the lease. Many times this term is used in the context of an SNDA.

- **Baseball Arbitration**: Form of arbitration where each party submits a proposal. In leasing this generally involves the rent rate; the context is typically in renewal clauses. The arbitrator chooses one submittal or the other. This methodology limits arbitrator's discretion. In theory this technique forces both parties to be reasonable in making proposals.

- **Base Rent**: The minimum rent due the landlord under the Lease. It is often coupled with provisions calling for its increase over the term. Sometimes this is referred to as "Basic Rent" or "Minimum Rent."

- **Base Year**: Specified year – typically the calendar year in which the lease commences. The taxes and Operating Expense for that year make up "Base Year" taxes/CAM etc. Example: Lease signed in 2018. Taxes that year are $5,000. If the Base Year is 2018 then all future years will be compared to that. So, if taxes in 2020 are $6,000 then the taxes due are $1,000.

- **Below Grade**: Structure or areas located below the surface grade – in other words – basement space. It is important to determine whether this is included in square footage.

- **Big Box**: a stand-alone retailer which resembles a large box and is in essence, a large warehouse building. Examples include Target, Home Depot, Wal-Mart and Ikea.

- **Blockchain**: A digitized and decentralized ledger which records and shares information across many computers. Because the record cannot be altered, leasing transactions and payment may be carried out more efficiently using this emerging technology.

- **BOMA**: This is the acronym for Building Owners & Managers Association. BOMA is known for publishing standards used in measuring space. These have become industry guidelines.

- **Breakpoint**: The threshold point for percentage rent to be payable by tenant. The number is obtained by dividing the annual Base Rent by the applicable percentage of sales. Thus, if the annual Base Rent is $60,000 and tenant and landlord have made a deal based on 6% of sales, the breakpoint is $1,000,000. If sales total $1,200,000 then the extra rent as a result of percentage rent is $200,000 x 6%, or $12,000/year.

- **Building Core**: Portions of the building that are not leased to tenants. The areas still provide value to the tenants. Items included are stairwells, elevators shafts, public restrooms, electrical distribution areas, etc. This is also known as a Load Factor.

- **Building Standard**: Specified construction materials and finishes established by a landlord as the basic quality standards for tenant improvements within the building. Examples include floor and wall coverings, lighting coverage, type and style of doors, partitioning etc. Sometimes these are spelled out in a written list. Often the landlord has a collection of samples and swatches which constitute Building Standard for tenant selection.

- **Build-out**: The construction of improvements to meet tenant specifications. Can include walls, flooring, electrical etc. Will often take into account the amount of Tenant Allowance provided in the lease.

- **Build-to-Suit**. Transaction in which the landlord will construct the space to the specifications required by the tenant. This may be a good way for the tenant to secure a space that fits its needs precisely without owning bricks and mortar.

- **Certificate of Occupancy ("C of O")**: Government generated form stating that the premises is legally ready to be occupied. Often lease commencement depends on the issuance of a C of O. Note: There can be temporary and final C of O documents.

- **Commencement Date:** The start date of the Lease Agreement.

- **Common Areas**: The areas of the particular building/project which are available for the non-exclusive use of all lessees. These can include lobbies, corridors, parking lots and equipment rooms.

- **Common Area Maintenance ("CAM")**: Charges paid by tenant for the upkeep and maintenance of Common Areas of the property. Examples include parking lot maintenance, snow removal, outdoor lighting, property taxes, and utilities. These are sometimes further classified into "controllable" and "non controllable" CAM items.

- **Concessions**: Inducements given by the landlord to tenant to sweeten the deal. Often these are free rent, tenant finish allowance, moving expenses, or similar items aimed at persuading tenant to sign. Some leases call for these to be paid back by tenant if tenant terminates early or defaults.

- **Comparables**: Often referred to as "Comps," these are rent rates and other key business terms for similar premises. These will help establish fair market rent rate for a lease in a similar local property.

- **Contiguous Space**: Space over one floor or connecting floors which can be combined and leased to a single tenant. Often, tenants will seek a first option or right of refusal on contiguous space.

- **Consumer Price Index**: ("CPI") Index prepared by the Bureau of Labor Statistics measuring cost of living. Used for calculating cost of living increase – typically to increase rent accordingly. There are several variations; the parties should clearly define which is to be used.

- **Controllables:** CAM items that are, at least in theory, within the reasonable control of the landlord. Typically these include all operating expenses except taxes, insurance, utilities and snow/ice removal.

- **Cross Default**: Provision which makes a default under one lease or agreement a default under another lease or agreement and vice-versa. Often used when tenant leases with two (2) different instruments or has a space leased by an affiliate.

- **Demising Wall**: The partition that separates one leased space from another leased premises or from the building's common areas like a public corridor. The Demising Wall creates the boundary of the premises. The location of a Demising Wall can significantly affect the amount of space and alter the Rent.

- **Early Termination Right**: A right generally granted to a tenant which allows it to end the Lease before the defined end of term. Often the tenant must pay a fee for this right. Sometimes, landlords reserve this right, particularly if they plan to make major improvements.

- **Escalation Clause**: Provision in which the rent is increased over time. Can be used to address changes in expenses paid such as real estate taxes, operating expenses etc., or to deal with inflation. Sometimes the calculation is based on a formula.

- **Eminent Domain**: Governmental right to condemn and acquire private property for public use in return for just compensation. This is addressed in the condemnation clause of the lease and can often involve issues as to access, parking field etc.

- **Encumbrance**: A charge, lien, claim, liability, or other matter which is binding on a property. Because it can affect the quality of title, it can have some resulting impact on the lease.

- **Estoppel Certificate**: Signed document which confirms that certain facts are true and correct as of a defined date. It is used and is to be relied upon by a third party like a purchaser or lender. Typically it verifies the major points (e.g., Base Rent, commencement and expiration, option availability) in the lease. The broker may be called upon to assist in obtaining this form.

- **Expense Stop:** Dollar amount of operating expenses, taxes and insurance generally expressed on a square foot basis) over which tenant pays its pro-rata share of increase. An example is in a building with a $6.00 expense stop, if the per square foot share of costs included in the expense stop is $6.50 a year, then the Tenant pays $.50 per foot for that year.

- **FASB**: Acronym for Financial Accounting Standards Board, a private organization which establishes financial accounting and reporting standards in the United States. New standards for FASB directly affect leasing because organizations now must include leases over one (1) year on their balance sheets.

- **First Refusal Right or Right of First Refusal (for purchase)**: Clause which gives tenant the first opportunity to buy the property at the same price and on the same terms and conditions as contained in a third party offer which the Landlord is willing to accept. This clause gives tenant the ability to control the property and buy it – although not at a fixed price.

- **First Refusal Right or Right of First Refusal (for lease)**: Clause affording tenant the first opportunity to lease additional space at the same price and on the same terms and conditions as those contained in a third party offer that landlord is willing to accept. This, like an option to expand, provides some assurance that tenant can have an opportunity to control additional space. It can also provide negotiating leverage for Tenants.

- **Flex Space**: Space allowing flexible use. Usually it is some combination which makes a premises able to be occupied as an office or showroom space, manufacturing, warehouse/distribution, etc. A tenant leasing Flex Space may want to make sure the Use Clause is also changeable. A Broker can sometimes creatively assist in the rebooting of traditional industrial space into flex space.

- **Force Majeure**: Clause which deals with events outside either party's control. Typically will apply in the lease to the acts of parties other than tenant payment. Often spelled out to include acts of God such as a flood, fire or weather, or acts of man like a strike, war etc. This provision will adjust time completion of a task, like a deadline for build out, in the light of specified uncontrollable events.

- **Forcible Entry and Detainer**: An action to regain possession if the existing Tenant does not vacate after notice. Basically another name for an eviction.

- **Go Dark:** The tenant's right to cease operation at its leased space while the tenant continues to pay rent. A Go Dark clause is commonly negotiated in retail leases. The right to Go Dark provides tenants with maximum flexibility, which is especially important for large national retail tenants.

- **Good Guy Guaranty**: A form of guaranty that is limited and covers only the period of time before the vacation of the space and surrender of the Premises. The Guaranty obligation ends once the space is given back so that the landlord can lease it to others.

- **Grace Period**: Additional time to satisfy an obligation before it ripens into a default. Generally applies to the time for payment.

- **Grey Shell:** A leasing/construction term for building space with an unfinished interior. This lacks ductwork and controls for HVAC and typically needs ceiling, lighting and plumbing as well as interior walls.

- **Gross Lease**: Lease in which the landlord agrees to pay all of the expenses associated with owning and operating the property. Thus, tenant pays a flat amount of rent. Landlord bears all expenses including insurance, maintenance, taxes and the like. Tenant is certain of a specified rent payment, and the landlord bears the risk of rising costs, unexpected expenditures etc. Sometimes, tenants pay utilities, but the lease is still called "Gross".

- **Gross Up Provision**: A clause that permits landlord to restate the Operating Expenses as if the Building is fully occupied (or sometimes a lesser percentage – like 95% occupied). This clause tends to shift responsibility for vacancies to tenant. By way of example, if electric isn't specifically metered, vacant space will use no electric. By grossing up, tenant loses the break it gets by averaging with vacant areas.

- **Ground Lease**: A lease of the land. Typically these run for a long time period. Many times these involve a building to be constructed on the property, like for example, a fast food restaurant. Often Ground Leases involve governmentally owned tracts, like land at an airport, etc.

- **Guaranty**: Typically required if the landlord is concerned about the credit of tenant. It is a legal agreement in which the guarantor assures satisfaction of tenant's debt or payment obligations. It sometimes extends to performance as well. There are many variations on the standard guaranty and some are limited to certain amounts or circumstances. For example, an individual may guaranty the first two (2) years of a lease or rent and obligations up to $25,000.

- **Hard Costs:** Construction expenditures for the actual physical construction. These include site costs, materials and labor – the brick-and-mortar expenditures.

- **Holdover:** Period of time space is occupied after the lease term has ended.

- **HVAC**: This is the acronym for heating, ventilating and air conditioning. Leases often focus on responsibility for this item because it is so central to the habitability of the space and can be a big ticket item.

- **Improvements:** Can refer to the physical work made to the building or site – either inside or outside.

- **Kick-out Clause:** Provision giving Tenant or Landlord opportunity to terminate a lease prior to the end of a term. Often called an early termination option.

- **Landlord's Lien**: A lien in favor of the landlord arising by operation of law or by contract. Tenants will typically have issues with these clauses and will want to strike them as they may interfere with ability to borrow.

- **Leasehold Improvements**: Improvements to the leased premises made by, and/or for, tenant. Can range from utilitarian to high end and will often affect the rent obligations.

- **Leasehold Interest:** The legal right to use property for a specified period of time.

- **Letter of Credit:** A Letter of Credit from a bank guaranteeing that a payment from one party to another will be received on time and for the correct amount, or that a performance will meet requirements. In the leasing context, sometimes if the tenant is unable to make payment, the letter of credit will be available to landlord.

- **Letter of Intent ("LOI"):** Preliminary outline of terms put together to structure a formal agreement.

- **Lifestyle Center**: Shopping center, many times of a streetscape design, which features specialty stores combined with other uses, often food and entertainment. Usually in an outdoor setting, it can be expanded to feature housing, hotel and office uses, with parks and other amenities.

- **Market Rent**: Rental income which a property would fetch on the open market with a landlord and a tenant ready and willing to lease in the ordinary course of business. Usually measured by recent lease transactions. Often this is a key measure in renewal clauses. The precise definition of market rent which is used in the document can significantly impact the rent paid during the renewal term.

- **Master Lease**: A document which is executed with the landlord giving the Master Tenant rights to control the entirety. The Master Tenant often will enter into leases with other entities for smaller space and terms so that those tenants are actual sublessees.

- **Mezzanine**: A floor located within the walls of the building that is capable of supporting offices, warehousing or other activities. It is above the ground floor and typically furnishes a view of the activities at floor level. Note: This has nothing to do with "mezzanine financing".

- **Mezzanine Financing**: In real estate it is a form of financing which is in the middle, falling between the senior debt (mortgage) and equity. It is subordinate and thus risker than a conventional mortgage and tends to cost more as a result.

- **Modified Gross Lease**: Kind of lease in which the tenant pays the initial base rent, but after the base years pays that rent plus a share of other costs – typically taxes, insurance, and Common Area Maintenance.

- **Net Lease**: A lease under which tenant pays costs associated with the operation of the property beyond the Base Rent. There are different levels and types of Net Leases. Terminology can be tricky. There can be significant differences between what one party thinks is Triple Net and the concept as understood by another. Here are some <u>general</u> approaches:
    o <u>Single Net Lease </u>(N) – Tenant pays property taxes. The landlord pays for all other expenses.

- - Double Net Lease (NN) – Tenant pays property taxes and insurance. The landlord pays for all other expenses.
  - Triple Net Lease (NNN) – Tenant pays the landlord Base Rent plus all other property-related expenses including taxes, insurance and maintenance. The landlord gets a true net payment; however, often this format calls for landlord to be responsible for roof and structure.
  - Bond Type – Tenant pays for everything, including all items of maintenance, replacement and repairs. Tenant pays rent to landlord like interest on a bond, every month regardless of ongoing issues.

- **Non-compete Clause**: Often called an "exclusivity" or an "exclusive use" clause. This is a provision specifying that tenant's business is exclusive in the property. It prohibits other tenants from operating the same or similar type of business in the property.

- **Non-controllables**: CAM expenses which are outside of landlord's reasonable control. Examples are utilities, taxes, insurance and snow and ice removal.

- **Occupancy Rate**: The percentage of units or area occupied at a particular point in time. The Occupancy Rate is 100% less the Vacancy Rate. If a building has 200 units and 100 are occupied it has an occupancy rate which is calculated by dividing 100/200 = 50%. Thus, if a property has a 75% Occupancy Rate, the Vacancy Rate is 25%.

- **Operating Expense Stop**: A negotiated point at which the landlord's contribution to Operating Expense ends. From tenant's position, it is the amount above which tenant is responsible for its Pro Rata share of Operating Expenses. Example: If the annual expense stop is $5.75, and expenses for the year are $7.00, then tenant pays $1.25 for that year.

- **Operating Expenses**: The costs involved in operating the property including maintenance, repairs, management, utilities, taxes and insurance. This definition can be subject to many exclusions.

- **Ordinary Wear and Tear**: The deterioration resulting from normal and reasonable use. Often tenant is not responsible to repair "ordinary wear and tear."

- **Parking Ratio**: A measure of the available parking. The Parking Ratio is usually expressed in particular spaces per 1000 feet of building space. Example: 8 parking spaces per 1000 feet. Certain businesses need a higher parking ratio. Call centers, for example, pack lots of workers, each with a car, in the most efficient space possible.

- **Percentage Lease**: Lease where certain rent is based on a percentage of the gross sales. The percentage lease is often used for restaurants and retail. There is usually a clause for a minimum rent as well. The existence of percentage rent can impact a number of other lease provisions, including the hours of operation, Go Dark and Radius Restriction.

- **Power Center**: A large outdoor shopping center with a shared parking lot and major "big box" stores, smaller retail stores and restaurants.

- **Pro Rata**: This term is used in various situations and refers to a proportionate share. One typical use is to refer to tenant's proportionate share of expenses for the maintenance and operation of the property.

- **Punch List**: An itemized list which lays out the incomplete or unsatisfactory items that require work after the premises is substantially complete. Generally, the lease will call for landlord to address punch list items promptly after tenant moves in.

- **Radius Restriction:** A provision that prohibits a tenant from establishing another location within a defined radius from the leased premises. This is particularly important in a Percentage Lease because it protects the percentage rental generated by that particular tenant.

- **Recapture**: A provision that allows a landlord to terminate the lease and get the space back. Often triggered in case of an Assignment request by tenant or can be triggered by bad performance of tenant.

For example a poorly performing Percentage Lease which is paying low percentage rents could be "recaptured."

- **Renewal Option:** Provision which gives tenant the right to extend the term of lease for a specified period of time.

- **Rent Commencement Date:** The date on which tenant begins Rent payments. This date can differ from the start date of the lease agreement.

- **Rent Concession:** A period of free or reduced rent provided as an inducement to the tenant.

- **Rentable Square Footage:** Means the Usable Square Footage plus tenant's Pro Rata share of the Building Common Areas, like lobbies, hallways and restrooms. Thus, Rentable Square Footage is a higher number and consequently tenant will share economic responsibility for "unusable" space.

- **Request for Proposal ("RFP"):** Summary submission laying out the major deal considerations of tenant. Generally, this is customized for specific needs. The RFP can be a powerful tool for tenant as it can be used to resolve multiple offers and obtain "apples to apples" comparisons.

- **Sale-Leaseback:** Transaction in which the owner sells a property and simultaneously enters into a lease to occupy as a tenant. The owner will have the use of the asset, but the technique frees up capital and may improve owner's balance sheet. Sometimes used for a short term to allow the buyer to earn a return while it leases up.

- **Security Deposit:** Money deposited by tenant to secure performance under the lease. Sometimes a Security Deposit is not cash, but a Letter of Credit or a promissory note. Large tenants will try to prevent the inclusion of a Security Deposit. Market norm can differ, but the Security Deposit is often one month's Rent.

- **Shadow Anchor:** A relationship where a retail Anchor Store serves the same purpose as a traffic generator and business driver to a nearby location.

- **Site Plan**: Drawing which locates improvements on the land. Many times this is a lease exhibit.

- **Site Selection.** The process of choosing the best location for an anticipated use. It includes identifying, evaluating, and assessing project needs in the context of the relative advantages and disadvantages of potential locations. The Site Selection process often consists of three phases: community evaluation; site analysis; and negotiation/selection.

- **Soft Costs**: Construction costs other than the Hard Costs. Soft Costs typically include legal, planning, architectural and engineering fees, commissions, financing costs etc.

- **Space Plan**: Plan setting out tenant's space requirements. The drawing typically identifies room sizes, Demising Walls, doors etc. Often there is a preliminary space plan which is developed into a final one during the lease negotiation process.

- **Staging**: The process of preparing a space for lease. Similar to home staging, but currently less likely to be used, it can be helpful in certain situations including shell office rental. This can be done through computer-generated graphics.

- **Sublease**: Agreement in which the original tenant (the "sublandlord") leases all or part of the Leasehold Interest to another party ("subtenant") while still retaining a Leasehold Interest in the property. Subleases may be complex because they involve extra considerations – the landlord's needs as well as those of the sublandlord and the subtenant.

- **Subordination and Non-disturbance Agreement ("SNDA")**: Agreement between tenant and landlord which allows lender's lien rights to become superior to those of the tenant, preserving tenant's rights to continue in occupancy if it pays rents even if a foreclosure occurs. It also provides that the tenant acknowledges and recognizes a new owner.

- **Tenant Improvements**: Improvement work performed on the space which can be paid for by landlord, tenant, or some combination, depending on the lease terms.

- **Tenant Improvement ("TI") Allowance**: The amount of money contributed by the landlord toward Tenant Improvements. Often, tenant pays costs that exceed the stipulated amount. Sometimes the TI Allowance is amortized and paid back as more rent over the term.

- **Tenant Mix:** The group of tenants that makes up a retail center and mixed use developments. Ideally an efficient tenant mix will maximize sales, stimulate business and lead to landlord prosperity. Tenant mix involves types of business and the location of the businesses in the physical space.

- **Termination Clause:** Lease provision that grants a party the power to terminate the lease.

- **Title Insurance**: Policy issued by a title insurance company providing coverage against loss resulting from defects of title or from the enforcement of liens existing when the title policy is issued. In larger lease transactions and ground leases some parties will wish to obtain a policy covering the Leasehold Interest.

- **Trade Fixtures**: Personal property attached to the structure used in the business. Since this personal property is part of the business rather than a part of real estate, usually it is removable upon lease termination.

- **Turnkey**: A phrase referencing a fully completed project. Often refers to a situation where landlord is responsible for the complete construction of tenant improvements, built to the customized specifications of tenant.

- **Use Clause**: Provision in a lease that sets out how the space can be utilized.

- **Usable Square Footage**: The area which is contained inside the demising walls of the premises. It is the space that is available for tenant's exclusive use. Thus, this is the space which excludes

Common Areas of the building like lobbies, restrooms, storage rooms etc.

- **Vacancy Rate**: The percentage of the total units or space that is vacant and thus available for occupancy at a particular point in time. For example, if a building has 200 units and 20 are empty then the Vacancy Rate is 20/200 = 10%.

- **Vanilla Box**: A leasing/construction shorthand term for the shell of a space with minimal finish. Generally, it means the ceiling and walls, plain concrete floor, electrical outlets, lighting, HVAC, and plumbing. Essentially space ready for the tenant's construction and finish.

- **Walkability**: A measure of how walker-friendly the property will be. Not only a measure of distance, but street patterns, amenities like parks, crime statistics, etc.

- **Work Letter**: Clause (usually an exhibit) to the lease which details the build-out of Tenant Improvements.

EXECUTIVE LEASE SUMMARY

(LEASE ABSTRACT)

      This Lease Summary is one example of what is sometimes called a lease digest or lease abstract. This can be an important form for owners and managers. You may also want to suggest it as a strategy template or an organizational form, regardless of whether you represent the Landlord or Tenant. You may also elect to keep it in your files for informational purposes and as a quick summary of terms. This form will also help to remind you of renewal timing and other such considerations after the execution of a Lease.

      Be aware that there are significant resources to assist in preparing lease abstracts. For example, there are companies that can provide abstracting services by trained lawyers or paralegals at very competitive prices. These vendors often use attorneys who now live overseas. Many are from top schools and from various reasons (spouse moved for job, etc.) do not practice in the United States, but can do work at reasonably low rates. Other companies use foreign-trained professionals and some even employ attorneys in the United States who no longer practice in the traditional way.

Lease Summary Form

GENERAL INFORMATION	
Property	
Suite/Premises	
Landlord Name	
Date Lease Signed (Landlord)	
Tenant Name	
Date Lease Signed (Tenant)	
Use	
Prohibited Uses	
Occupancy Start	
Rent Start	
Effective Date	
Commencement Date	
Expiration Date	
Lease Term	
Rentable Area	
Usable Area	
Tenant's Prorata Share %	

RENTAL INFORMATION	
Initial Base Rent	
Months	
Rent/SF	
Monthly Rent	
Annual Rent	
Rental Adjustments During Term	
Adjustment Date	
Adjusted Base Rent/SF	
Adjusted Monthly Rent	
Rental Abatement	
Lease Concessions	
Initial Estimated Operating Expenses	
CAM	
Insurance	
Operating Expenses Increase Provisions	
Security Deposit	

GUARANTOR AND NOTICE	
Guarantor(s)	
Landlord's Notice Address	
Copy To	
Tenant's Notice Address	
Copy To	

EXHIBITS AND OPTIONS	
Exhibits to Lease	
Renewal Option(s)	
Notification Date(s)	
Terms	
Expansion Option(s)	
Location	
Terms	
Termination Option(s)	
Notification Date	
Terms	
Relocation Option by Landlord	
Notification Date	
Early Termination Option	

OTHER	
Parking	
Exclusive Use	
Assignment and Subletting	
Holding Over	
Estimated Construction Costs	
Total Costs	
Cost/SF	
Tenant To Pay Extra Cost	
Allowance Costs	
Cost/SF	
Amortization	
Signage	
Alterations	
Tenant Broker(s)	
Landlord Broker(s)	
Details Of Commission(s)	
Details Of Any Commission After Move-In	
Other Clauses/Terms	

COMMERCIAL LEASE CONTACT LIST

One of the themes of this book is the need to be organized in order to get the most done in the least time. This Contact List is a simple means of keeping the key information at your fingertips. There are plenty of more "technologically-advanced" ways of data organization – see Section V for programs or resources that can help.

> **Tip:**
>
> **Build a Toolkit.** When you see a problem brilliantly solved or you figure out an easy fix to a better deal point – write it down. Keep a computer folder or 3 ring binder full of good clauses and language. When you face a similar issue five years down the road, you don't have to research for what the heck you did, or worse – scratch your head wondering where you faced that one before.

Commercial Lease Contact List Form

CONTACTS	
Landlord Contact	
Firm Name:	
Address:	
Email:	
Phone:	
Fax:	
Landlord Broker	
Firm Name:	
Address:	
Email:	
Phone:	
Fax:	
Landlord Counsel	
Firm Name:	
Address:	
Email:	
Phone:	
Fax:	
Tenant Contact	
Firm Name:	
Address:	
Email:	
Phone:	
Fax:	
Tenant Broker	
Firm Name:	
Address:	
Email:	
Phone:	
Fax:	

Tenant Counsel	
Firm Name:	
Address:	
Email:	
Phone:	
Fax:	
Architect	
Firm Name:	
Address:	
Email:	
Phone:	
Fax:	
Space Planner	
Firm Name:	
Address:	
Email:	
Phone:	
Fax:	
Environmental Consultant	
Firm Name:	
Address:	
Email:	
Phone:	
Fax:	
Geotechnical Consultant	
Firm Name:	
Address:	
Email:	
Phone:	
Fax:	
Structural Consultant	
Firm Name:	
Address:	
Email:	
Phone:	
Fax:	

Surveyor	
Firm Name:	
Address:	
Email:	
Phone:	
Fax:	
Relocation Firm	
Firm Name:	
Address:	
Email:	
Phone:	
Fax:	
Landlord Insurance Agent	
Firm Name:	
Address:	
Email:	
Phone:	
Fax:	
Tenant Insurance Agent	
Firm Name:	
Address:	
Email:	
Phone:	
Fax:	
Other	
Firm Name:	
Address:	
Email:	
Phone:	
Fax:	
Other	
Firm Name:	
Address:	
Email:	
Phone:	
Fax:	

COMPETITIVE ADVANTAGES

The Competitive Advantages Form provided permits a Broker to identify how his property stacks up against competitive listings. Information is organized in a usable fashion. The form may also be used to figure out an appropriate rate or to educate an unrealistic owner on the real-world issues faced by a less than ideal site.

This form may also be used or adapted by a Broker representing a tenant to compare multiple sites. Further, this form can be freely revised to cover other issues. Blank sections are left for customization.

Two examples of this form are provided. The first does not "score"; in other words, the first form merely summarizes information and judgments about a property. The other actually scores the listings so that a quantitative scorecard is created. Some may choose to "weight" the scoring to be even more analytical – the more points, the more important etc.

Technological advances are making extremely rich and helpful information available to parties almost instantaneously. Some professionals may take advantage of publicly available or proprietary sources to generate sophisticated studies. Many are variations on, or improvements of, those included here. Please look at some of the resources in Section V since they may make your life much easier and your work even better. Familiarize yourself with issues like those highlighted here so you can approach your work in a sophisticated and professional way.

Competitive Advantages Form

ITEM	LISTED PROPERY	COMPETITIVE LISTING A	COMPETITIVE LISTING B	COMPETITIVE LISTING C
Address				
City				
Submarket				
Distance from Listed Property				
Price/Sq. Ft.				
Type of Property				
Square Footage				
Total Square Footage				
Type of Lease				
Construction				
CAM				
Utilities				
Type of Heating				
Type of AC				
Location				
Age of Building				
Single Tenant or Multi-Tenant				

COMPARATIVE CHARACTERISTICS	COMPETITIVE LISTING A	COMPETITIVE LISTING B	COMPETITIVE LISTING C
Restrooms	☐ Better ☐ Similar ☐ Inferior	☐ Better ☐ Similar ☐ Inferior	☐ Better ☐ Similar ☐ Inferior
Landlord Incentives	☐ Better ☐ Similar ☐ Inferior	☐ Better ☐ Similar ☐ Inferior	☐ Better ☐ Similar ☐ Inferior
Amenities	☐ Better ☐ Similar ☐ Inferior	☐ Better ☐ Similar ☐ Inferior	☐ Better ☐ Similar ☐ Inferior
Parking	☐ Better ☐ Similar ☐ Inferior	☐ Better ☐ Similar ☐ Inferior	☐ Better ☐ Similar ☐ Inferior
Expansion Availability	☐ Better ☐ Similar ☐ Inferior	☐ Better ☐ Similar ☐ Inferior	☐ Better ☐ Similar ☐ Inferior
Property Characteristics	☐ Better ☐ Similar ☐ Inferior	☐ Better ☐ Similar ☐ Inferior	☐ Better ☐ Similar ☐ Inferior
Floor Plans	☐ Better ☐ Similar ☐ Inferior	☐ Better ☐ Similar ☐ Inferior	☐ Better ☐ Similar ☐ Inferior
Exterior Condition	☐ Better ☐ Similar ☐ Inferior	☐ Better ☐ Similar ☐ Inferior	☐ Better ☐ Similar ☐ Inferior
Interior Condition	☐ Better ☐ Similar ☐ Inferior	☐ Better ☐ Similar ☐ Inferior	☐ Better ☐ Similar ☐ Inferior
Tenant Mix	☐ Better ☐ Similar ☐ Inferior	☐ Better ☐ Similar ☐ Inferior	☐ Better ☐ Similar ☐ Inferior
Signage	☐ Better ☐ Similar ☐ Inferior	☐ Better ☐ Similar ☐ Inferior	☐ Better ☐ Similar ☐ Inferior
Median Household Income within Five Miles	☐ Better ☐ Similar ☐ Inferior	☐ Better ☐ Similar ☐ Inferior	☐ Better ☐ Similar ☐ Inferior
Walkability	☐ Better ☐ Similar ☐ Inferior	☐ Better ☐ Similar ☐ Inferior	☐ Better ☐ Similar ☐ Inferior

COMPARATIVE CHARACTERISTICS	COMPETITIVE LISTING A	COMPETITIVE LISTING B	COMPETITIVE LISTING C
Public Transportation	☐ Better ☐ Similar ☐ Inferior	☐ Better ☐ Similar ☐ Inferior	☐ Better ☐ Similar ☐ Inferior
Proximity to Management Residential	☐ Better ☐ Similar ☐ Inferior	☐ Better ☐ Similar ☐ Inferior	☐ Better ☐ Similar ☐ Inferior
Proximity to Employee Residential	☐ Better ☐ Similar ☐ Inferior	☐ Better ☐ Similar ☐ Inferior	☐ Better ☐ Similar ☐ Inferior
Major Highway Access	☐ Better ☐ Similar ☐ Inferior	☐ Better ☐ Similar ☐ Inferior	☐ Better ☐ Similar ☐ Inferior
Docks/Loading	☐ Better ☐ Similar ☐ Inferior	☐ Better ☐ Similar ☐ Inferior	☐ Better ☐ Similar ☐ Inferior
Visibility to Traffic	☐ Better ☐ Similar ☐ Inferior	☐ Better ☐ Similar ☐ Inferior	☐ Better ☐ Similar ☐ Inferior
Architecture of Building	☐ Better ☐ Similar ☐ Inferior	☐ Better ☐ Similar ☐ Inferior	☐ Better ☐ Similar ☐ Inferior
Building Recognition	☐ Better ☐ Similar ☐ Inferior	☐ Better ☐ Similar ☐ Inferior	☐ Better ☐ Similar ☐ Inferior
Naming Rights	☐ Better ☐ Similar ☐ Inferior	☐ Better ☐ Similar ☐ Inferior	☐ Better ☐ Similar ☐ Inferior
Location of Competition	☐ Better ☐ Similar ☐ Inferior	☐ Better ☐ Similar ☐ Inferior	☐ Better ☐ Similar ☐ Inferior
Proximity to Customers/Clients	☐ Better ☐ Similar ☐ Inferior	☐ Better ☐ Similar ☐ Inferior	☐ Better ☐ Similar ☐ Inferior
Proximity to Suppliers	☐ Better ☐ Similar ☐ Inferior	☐ Better ☐ Similar ☐ Inferior	☐ Better ☐ Similar ☐ Inferior
Proximity to Food/Restaurants	☐ Better ☐ Similar ☐ Inferior	☐ Better ☐ Similar ☐ Inferior	☐ Better ☐ Similar ☐ Inferior

COMPARATIVE CHARACTERISTICS	COMPETITIVE LISTING A	COMPETITIVE LISTING B	COMPETITIVE LISTING C
Green/LEED	☐ Better ☐ Similar ☐ Inferior	☐ Better ☐ Similar ☐ Inferior	☐ Better ☐ Similar ☐ Inferior
Energy Efficiency	☐ Better ☐ Similar ☐ Inferior	☐ Better ☐ Similar ☐ Inferior	☐ Better ☐ Similar ☐ Inferior
Gross Rent	☐ Better ☐ Similar ☐ Inferior	☐ Better ☐ Similar ☐ Inferior	☐ Better ☐ Similar ☐ Inferior
Economic Incentives	☐ Better ☐ Similar ☐ Inferior	☐ Better ☐ Similar ☐ Inferior	☐ Better ☐ Similar ☐ Inferior
OVERALL RATING	☐ Better ☐ Similar ☐ Inferior	☐ Better ☐ Similar ☐ Inferior	☐ Better ☐ Similar ☐ Inferior
NOTES AND COMMENTS			

Competitive Advantages Form (With Numbers)

ITEM	LISTED PROPERTY	COMPETITIVE LISTING A	COMPETITIVE LISTING B	COMPETITIVE LISTING C
Address				
City				
Submarket				
Distance from Listed Property				
Price/Sq. Ft.				
Type of Property				
Square Footage				
Total Square Footage				
Type of Lease				
Construction				
CAM				
Utilities				
Type of Heating				
Type of AC				
Location				
Age of Building				
Single Tenant or Multi-Tenant				

COMPARATIVE CHARACTERISTICS	COMPETITIVE LISTING A	COMPETITIVE LISTING B	COMPETITIVE LISTING C
Restrooms	☐ Better = 3 ☐ Similar = 2 ☐ Inferior =1	☐ Better = 3 ☐ Similar = 2 ☐ Inferior =1	☐ Better = 3 ☐ Similar = 2 ☐ Inferior =1
Landlord Incentives	☐ Better = 3 ☐ Similar = 2 ☐ Inferior =1	☐ Better = 3 ☐ Similar = 2 ☐ Inferior =1	☐ Better = 3 ☐ Similar = 2 ☐ Inferior =1
Amenities	☐ Better = 3 ☐ Similar = 2 ☐ Inferior =1	☐ Better = 3 ☐ Similar = 2 ☐ Inferior =1	☐ Better = 3 ☐ Similar = 2 ☐ Inferior =1
Parking	☐ Better = 3 ☐ Similar = 2 ☐ Inferior =1	☐ Better = 3 ☐ Similar = 2 ☐ Inferior =1	☐ Better = 3 ☐ Similar = 2 ☐ Inferior =1
Expansion Availability	☐ Better = 3 ☐ Similar = 2 ☐ Inferior =1	☐ Better = 3 ☐ Similar = 2 ☐ Inferior =1	☐ Better = 3 ☐ Similar = 2 ☐ Inferior =1
Property Characteristics	☐ Better = 3 ☐ Similar = 2 ☐ Inferior =1	☐ Better = 3 ☐ Similar = 2 ☐ Inferior =1	☐ Better = 3 ☐ Similar = 2 ☐ Inferior =1
Floor Plans	☐ Better = 3 ☐ Similar = 2 ☐ Inferior =1	☐ Better = 3 ☐ Similar = 2 ☐ Inferior =1	☐ Better = 3 ☐ Similar = 2 ☐ Inferior =1
Exterior Condition	☐ Better = 3 ☐ Similar = 2 ☐ Inferior =1	☐ Better = 3 ☐ Similar = 2 ☐ Inferior =1	☐ Better = 3 ☐ Similar = 2 ☐ Inferior =1
Interior Condition	☐ Better = 3 ☐ Similar = 2 ☐ Inferior =1	☐ Better = 3 ☐ Similar = 2 ☐ Inferior =1	☐ Better = 3 ☐ Similar = 2 ☐ Inferior =1
Tenant Mix	☐ Better = 3 ☐ Similar = 2 ☐ Inferior =1	☐ Better = 3 ☐ Similar = 2 ☐ Inferior =1	☐ Better = 3 ☐ Similar = 2 ☐ Inferior =1
Signage	☐ Better = 3 ☐ Similar = 2 ☐ Inferior =1	☐ Better = 3 ☐ Similar = 2 ☐ Inferior =1	☐ Better = 3 ☐ Similar = 2 ☐ Inferior =1
Median Household Income within Five Miles	☐ Better = 3 ☐ Similar = 2 ☐ Inferior =1	☐ Better = 3 ☐ Similar = 2 ☐ Inferior =1	☐ Better = 3 ☐ Similar = 2 ☐ Inferior =1
Walkability	☐ Better = 3 ☐ Similar = 2 ☐ Inferior =1	☐ Better = 3 ☐ Similar = 2 ☐ Inferior =1	☐ Better = 3 ☐ Similar = 2 ☐ Inferior =1

COMPARATIVE CHARACTERISTICS	COMPETITIVE LISTING A	COMPETITIVE LISTING B	COMPETITIVE LISTING C
Public Transportation	☐ Better = 3 ☐ Similar = 2 ☐ Inferior =1	☐ Better = 3 ☐ Similar = 2 ☐ Inferior =1	☐ Better = 3 ☐ Similar = 2 ☐ Inferior =1
Proximity to Management Residential	☐ Better = 3 ☐ Similar = 2 ☐ Inferior =1	☐ Better = 3 ☐ Similar = 2 ☐ Inferior =1	☐ Better = 3 ☐ Similar = 2 ☐ Inferior =1
Proximity to Employee Residential	☐ Better = 3 ☐ Similar = 2 ☐ Inferior =1	☐ Better = 3 ☐ Similar = 2 ☐ Inferior =1	☐ Better = 3 ☐ Similar = 2 ☐ Inferior =1
Major Highway Access	☐ Better = 3 ☐ Similar = 2 ☐ Inferior =1	☐ Better = 3 ☐ Similar = 2 ☐ Inferior =1	☐ Better = 3 ☐ Similar = 2 ☐ Inferior =1
Docks/Loading	☐ Better = 3 ☐ Similar = 2 ☐ Inferior =1	☐ Better = 3 ☐ Similar = 2 ☐ Inferior =1	☐ Better = 3 ☐ Similar = 2 ☐ Inferior =1
Visibility to Traffic	☐ Better = 3 ☐ Similar = 2 ☐ Inferior =1	☐ Better = 3 ☐ Similar = 2 ☐ Inferior =1	☐ Better = 3 ☐ Similar = 2 ☐ Inferior =1
Architecture of Building	☐ Better = 3 ☐ Similar = 2 ☐ Inferior =1	☐ Better = 3 ☐ Similar = 2 ☐ Inferior =1	☐ Better = 3 ☐ Similar = 2 ☐ Inferior =1
Building Recognition	☐ Better = 3 ☐ Similar = 2 ☐ Inferior =1	☐ Better = 3 ☐ Similar = 2 ☐ Inferior =1	☐ Better = 3 ☐ Similar = 2 ☐ Inferior =1
Naming Rights	☐ Better = 3 ☐ Similar = 2 ☐ Inferior =1	☐ Better = 3 ☐ Similar = 2 ☐ Inferior =1	☐ Better = 3 ☐ Similar = 2 ☐ Inferior =1
Location of Competition	☐ Better = 3 ☐ Similar = 2 ☐ Inferior =1	☐ Better = 3 ☐ Similar = 2 ☐ Inferior =1	☐ Better = 3 ☐ Similar = 2 ☐ Inferior =1
Proximity to Customers/Clients	☐ Better = 3 ☐ Similar = 2 ☐ Inferior =1	☐ Better = 3 ☐ Similar = 2 ☐ Inferior =1	☐ Better = 3 ☐ Similar = 2 ☐ Inferior =1
Proximity to Suppliers	☐ Better = 3 ☐ Similar = 2 ☐ Inferior =1	☐ Better = 3 ☐ Similar = 2 ☐ Inferior =1	☐ Better = 3 ☐ Similar = 2 ☐ Inferior =1
Proximity to Food/Restaurants	☐ Better = 3 ☐ Similar = 2 ☐ Inferior =1	☐ Better = 3 ☐ Similar = 2 ☐ Inferior =1	☐ Better = 3 ☐ Similar = 2 ☐ Inferior =1

COMPARATIVE CHARACTERISTICS	COMPETITIVE LISTING A	COMPETITIVE LISTING B	COMPETITIVE LISTING C
Green/LEED	☐ Better = 3 ☐ Similar = 2 ☐ Inferior =1	☐ Better = 3 ☐ Similar = 2 ☐ Inferior =1	☐ Better = 3 ☐ Similar = 2 ☐ Inferior =1
Energy Efficiency	☐ Better = 3 ☐ Similar = 2 ☐ Inferior =1	☐ Better = 3 ☐ Similar = 2 ☐ Inferior =1	☐ Better = 3 ☐ Similar = 2 ☐ Inferior =1
Gross Rent	☐ Better = 3 ☐ Similar = 2 ☐ Inferior =1	☐ Better = 3 ☐ Similar = 2 ☐ Inferior =1	☐ Better = 3 ☐ Similar = 2 ☐ Inferior =1
Economic Incentives	☐ Better = 3 ☐ Similar = 2 ☐ Inferior =1	☐ Better = 3 ☐ Similar = 2 ☐ Inferior =1	☐ Better = 3 ☐ Similar = 2 ☐ Inferior =1
OVERALL RATING	Total _____	Total _____	Total _____

NOTES AND COMMENTS

NEGOTIATION SKILLS

We can hardly scratch the surface in this area. There are books, seminars and courses that will help you learn to succeed in negotiation. A few paragraphs is only a drive off the first tee. Still, you will never be a great success as a commercial Broker without some ability to negotiate – and to do so in a way that does not burn bridges, but builds them for the future.

1. **You Should Not Expect To Win Everything**. In fact, you will do better if you lose a few less important issues. After all, everybody wants to win and the people sitting on the other side of the lease negotiation will undoubtedly want to feel successful too. Be conscious of what is really important and what you can afford to "give away". Naturally, no giveaway can be made without the authority of your client. Be prepared to educate your client and to demonstrate why you feel an issue is rather unimportant and worth "losing".

2. **Know More About The Deal Than They Do**. Gather all the facts. Even round up rumors. Perhaps the landlord is extremely arrogant or stubborn and he or she will never give on rent rate. Think about what you can propose to keep the rent rate where he or she wants it and still get a good deal for the tenant. More Tenant Improvements? Kick-out Clause? Does the other party have viable options? If not, you can be more obstinate. Knowing a lot can help your client tremendously.

3. **Be Professional and Stay Cool.** Even if the other side starts taking cheap shots, refrain from that behavior. Keep your cool. Let's say that they start blaming you for misinformation and delay. If it's true, admit your fault and clear the air; if it's not, then defend yourself politely and move on. Don't get bitter or take cheap shots. People on the other side may be under tremendous pressure. They may have personal problems eating at them. Try to take the high road. It should generally get you there better than getting down into trench warfare.

4. **Be Bold – Ask for Things**. As we mention in the material entitled "Good Asks", we generally find that being assertive and asking for concessions yields more than assuming the worst and failing to ask. It's amazing what you can sometimes do if you simply ask for it. This does not mean you should be ridiculously demanding or be asking for what is patently unfair. But, a well-informed negotiator who keeps his or her eyes and ears open and knows what is really important for the other side can figure out what may simply pass under the radar and benefit his or her client.

5. **Listen, Listen, Listen**. If the other side talks, see what is really important to them. When the tenant is constantly talking about "move in date" and you realize they have no place to go, you can try to meet their needs, and at the same time focus on what they want, you can make them feel they are being heard. When you help them solve their problem – by being creative and gracious, they will tend to give you things – often things that make the deal happen.

6. **Recognize The Time Schedules**. Some deals happen fast. Some deals take a long time. If you are year away from termination and you are negotiating a renewal, pay attention to the term of the old lease. When is notice due? What is the market like? Is landlord doing well or in trouble? Learn when to push and when to be patient. If Broker also fails to understand that both lawyers are just plain slow, it will look bad if he constantly pesters them. And remember that sometimes your client will want to move slowly. Perhaps there are reasons why they want to keep their options open and not move too fast. Be alert. Explore the deal in context to better understand your tactical role.

SECTION II: REPRESENTING THE LANDLORD

"Act as if what you do makes a difference. It does."

~ William James

INTRODUCTION TO REPRESENTING THE LANDLORD

The Broker is a key collaborator with the landlord. A good agent plays a far greater role beyond merely placing a sign or mailing out a listing. By learning the market, the property, the competition, and the issues, the Broker can advise the owner in a manner that can lead to tangible financial gains and a reduction of risks.

While each deal can have its own peculiarities, the following usually apply to most commercial Landlord/Broker transactions:

a. <u>Analysis of the Property</u>. Work to understand the property as a whole and the premises in particular. Gather all the key information about construction, amenities, lease expenditures, etc. so that any question can be answered quickly and in an organized manner. By having this data upfront, you not only make the leasing process quicker, but you also strengthen your own position as the likely listing Broker. Simply put – you will know so much and have so much information at your fingertips that you will be ready to perform in connection with the particular asset.

b. <u>Understand the Competition</u>. There are occasional opportunities where your property is the one and only – there really is no competition. For example, if you have the only move-in ready refrigerated space in the region and the prospect needs refrigeration immediately, then the competition doesn't count for much. Usually, however, that is not the case. More often than not, you will need to be able to advise the landlord on the strengths and weaknesses of the competition. This will not only assist the landlord in getting realistic leases to the finish line, but it will also give you the ability to educate the owner on exactly what she is up against. An owner who thinks that she has the crown jewel asset occasionally needs to be brought down to earth. If the competing spaces are better, cheaper, or are offering free rent, then the landlord had better get herself in a mode to be competitive by offering aggressive incentives.

c. <u>Comparables</u>. Once you are up-to-speed on the nuts and bolts of your property and have a reasonable assessment of the competition, you need to pull together a history of what has been going on in the market. Use the available information online and use your in-house resources as well in order to check out recent transactions. You do not want to seek $17.00 per square foot when the going rate is $12.00 per square foot, and you don't want to offer move-in allowances that are far greater than the competition's unless you and the owner believe that this is a key differentiation technique.

d. <u>Build a Strategy</u>. Armed with the deep understanding of the market and the property, you can guide the landlord into deals. You will want to especially concentrate on determining the identity of prospective tenants, where they can be found, and what kind of pricing strategy should be offered. The development of this strategy is a mix of art and science. Experience in the field will likely make you better and better. If you are a novice or you are venturing into a specialty which is outside of your comfort level, you should reach out to other agents and mentors to shape a plan. Use common sense and don't be afraid to brainstorm. If you have a difficult space, expand your target prospects to the ones who you might otherwise overlook. Be creative.

e. <u>Marketing</u>. A paragraph or so here will not, by any means make you a successful marketer, although the resources we have included in Section V may provide quantum leap in your marketing skills and put powerful tools in your hands. In addition, we have provided a marketing management summary which may start you on a marketing program. Further improvements can come from hard work and diligence. Go to seminars and learn from others. Check out websites and circulars from others. What strikes you about the materials, events, and/or books at conventions? What do you think makes the biggest impact? Consider questions like these, and then tailor your message to the particular property so that it sends the right message. If you have marketing professionals working for your brokerage, use their skills to improve your presentation for the strategy of the property.

f. Networking. You can be the smartest and most diligent broker, but ultimately you need clients. Try to connect with other brokers in your area. Many cities have real estate specific meet ups that will connect you with potential clients who are wanting to do deals and other brokers who may help you land a client in the future.

g. Lease Negotiations – Pre-Document Stage. It may help to view lease negotiations as a two-part process. The initial stage focuses on the lease preparation/LOI/RFP. It is here where many early wins can make a good deal into a better one. On the other hand, sloppiness and lack of attention to detail in the early stages can kill a deal.

   This process is often rushed because it is non-binding, and the landlord and lawyers are not always as careful as they should be. Use your skills to stay one step ahead of the tenant, but avoid the impression that the landlord is difficult or inflexible. Try to have solutions in advance for anticipated problems. By way of example, think about a situation where the landlord has an empty large room in a shopping center. You have secured a prospective tenant who wants a Right of First Refusal ("ROFR") on adjacent space and has inserted language in the LOI that would give the tenant the right to meet offers for adjacent space, but made the ROFR contemporaneous with the tenant's term. This means the landlord could lose deals and fresh tenant mix opportunities to very short term tenancies by "new" prospects late in the tenant's lease term. You can suggest that the owner insert language that will require the tenant to extend its lease if it meets the ROFR so that the original lease space and the adjacent space end contemporaneously, but no earlier than the date in the ROFR. Also, if at all possible, try to control the documents.

h. Lease Negotiations – Document Stage. As you know, you want to absolutely avoid giving legal advice. You should know your boundaries. Hopefully, you will have the assistance of a good real estate lawyer who can assist you. However, you don't have to be kicked to the sidelines.

   Here are some of the tasks which you will be expected to carry out:

- Check the Proposal/LOI against the Lease. Are the business terms correct? Are the dates right? Is the brokerage covered?
- Work with the owner and counsel to negotiate the documents. Help where you can to avoid disputes and try to come up with solutions.
- If the property is specialized, see if you can come up with industry-specific solutions. For example, if the landlord is called upon by the tenant to provide a level lot, obtain grading standards.
- Save legal costs and time by focusing on all the key elements. Try to get the agents and parties, especially the broker for the tenant, to remove the issues which are simply unreasonable or non-starters.
- Coordinate (where possible) the activities of counsel, space planners, contractors, etc.
- Provide good references based on your experience. If a tenant needs someone to do its buildout, give the name of a quality contractor.
- Help to avoid mistakes. Pay attention to detail.

INTERVIEW AND QUALIFICATION OF A PROSPECTIVE LESSEE

Typically, a prospective tenant will need to be qualified. The process can vary based on a number of factors. The following is a series of suggestions/questions to help organize the process of qualifying the prospect and getting the file started.

Also, while this particular document is set up for a Landlord Broker, it is obviously appropriate for Tenant Brokers too. Indeed, the Tenant Broker must almost be more committed to the process of vetting, and for the Tenant representative, it can be a two way process. The Broker naturally is checking out the prospective client and confirming its ability to perform and that the use of the property adheres does and does not affect the future value. At the same time the prospect is vetting the Broker. Does the Broker understand its needs? Does the Broker have the necessary expertise?

Using the right process and form will not only allow the Broker to get the job, but to tackle it in an efficient way. A prospect which does not feel pressure and senses that it is working with an organized and quality professional will be more likely to hire that professional to do the work.

If you or one of your managers decide that a prospective tenant is not appropriate for a space, then you need to document the reasons in a manner that is consistent with applicable law. Discrimination is totally unacceptable. Always get expert advice.

PROSPECTIVE TENANT SUMMARY

1. **THRESHOLD CONSIDERATIONS**

    -Is the Prospect creditworthy?

    - Credit Reports?
    - References?
    - If private entity, can it provide financials?
    - Previous landlord – any problems?

    -Is the Prospect serious?
    - What is their current status? Lease ending? Selling property?
    - Is there a true interest or is this a fishing expedition?
    - Are other firms being considered?

2. **DECISION MAKERS AND CONTACT PERSONS**

    - Who decides on representation?
    - Who is going to make the decision as to the ultimate transaction?
    - Will decision be made by persons who will be on-site?
    - Who is the contact person for the assignment?
    - Who is the contract person for the transaction itself?

3. **EXPECTATIONS**

    - What is the prospect looking for?
    - What is the Broker expected to do?
    - Are there special requirements?
    - Does prospective client understand the process?

4. **GEOGRAPHY/LOCATION**

    - Is the general area already selected or is there a wish list?

- Does entity want to stay in the area?
- If already in area – how near to existing facility?
  - Where are prospect's clients and customers?
  - Where are prospect's suppliers?
- Key needs as to location?
  - Rooftops
  - Roads/Access
  - Airport
  - Railroad
  - Proximity to suppliers
  - Visibility
  - Parking
  - Storage
- Public transportation?
- Where do the key decision makers live?
- Are incentives important?

5. TIMING

- How much time is left on present lease? (if leased)
- Are there certain times of year in which prospect cannot move?
- What is the target date for lease?
- What is the target date for move in?

6. MOTIVATION AND GAINS

- Is Prospect in the market now?
- Is this an expansion or is it a new business?
- What does prospect like about current location?
- What does prospect dislike about current location?

7. RENT/COST/ECOMOMICS

- What kind of Rents? Increases acceptable? How much?

- How long of a term? Options?
- Size of space is needed?
- Expansion needs?
- Special requirements?
- Build-out cost?
- Need for relocation services?

LISTING AGREEMENTS

Getting a listing is obviously the first step, but getting the details in writing and in a way is fair and clear to both sides is key. Naturally, you may have an in-house form that your company requires. If, however, you have the opportunity or need to depart from that, or if your client is uncomfortable with that document, you may wish to consider forms like these.

Form 1

This is a rather formal and generally comprehensive Listing Agreement between an Owner and Broker.

Several notes about this particular form:

Blanks are to be filled out based upon the agreement of the parties. Commission for example, is to be inserted. Many Brokers will have a term sheet they like to use and which can be attached as an exhibit and thus integrated into the form.

Also, this form has a blank to be filled in with the general lease terms. (See Section 2) The parties may want to prepare an exhibit with details for this too.

DO NOT ADOPT THIS, OR ANY OTHER CONTRACTUAL FORM, WITHOUT CONSULTING YOUR ATTORNEY TO MAKE SURE THAT IT IS APPROPRIATE FOR YOUR PRACTICE AND APPLICABLE STATE LAW. FURTHER, YOU MUST MAKE SURE YOUR BROKER HAS APPROVED THE USE OF THAT DOCUMENT.

Form 2

This is a long Form Listing Agreement between the owner and a Broker for leasing services. It contains two schedules. Schedule 1 contains the prospective lease terms and Schedule 2 stipulates the commission amounts. The Agreement has blanks and blocks to be checked, and like Form 1 requires review and assistance from counsel before you adopt it.

Form 1

LISTING AGREEMENT

This Listing Agreement (this "Agreement") is dated as of _____, 20____, ("Effective Date") by and between _____ (the "Broker") and _____ (the "Owner").

RECITALS

    A.   Owner owns real property located at _____, as improved (the buildings, improvements, associated facilities and real property are collectively referred to as the "Property").

    B.   Owner seeks one or more tenant(s) for the Property.

    C.   Broker is a duly licensed real estate broker in the State of _____.

NOW, THEREFORE, in consideration of the premises and the mutual covenants and agreements herein set forth, Broker and Owner hereby agree as follows:

    1.   <u>Term.</u> This Agreement is for a term beginning on _____ and ending _____, unless extended in writing by Owner.

    2.   <u>Exclusive Listing.</u> Owner grants Broker an exclusive right to offer the Property for lease on the following terms: _____ Owner shall have the right to verify the credit and net worth of any prospective tenant. Any lease terms which are not specifically set out in this Agreement (or in subsequent written directions from Owner to Broker) are subject to the prior approval of Owner.

3. <u>Commission</u>. If a Lease is executed prior to the termination of this Agreement (or after termination pursuant to Section 5 below), Owner agrees that Broker shall have earned a commission. Commission under this Agreement is as follows: _____

4. <u>Lease Agreements</u>. All proposed agreements for the lease of the Property shall be made in Owner's name, and on the terms and conditions acceptable to Owner both as to form and substance. Broker has no authority to enter into any agreement for the lease of the Property for or on behalf of Owner. Broker's limited authority under this Agreement is to perform its services and solicit lease offers from bona fide third parties.

5. <u>Prospects</u>. Within 15 days after the end of the term of this Agreement, or if this Agreement is sooner terminated within 15 days following such date of termination, Broker shall designate in writing (a) each party with whom Broker had significant contacts in its effort to solicit and obtain offers to lease the Property during the term of this Agreement, and (b) the nature and status of the negotiations with such prospects. Each party so designated and specified in the notice is a "Broker's Prospect." If Owner executes and enters into an agreement for the lease of the Property (or any part thereof) with any Broker's Prospect within _____ days after the expiration or termination of this Agreement, Broker shall be entitled to the same commission payable in accordance with Section 3.

6. <u>Cooperating Brokers</u>. Broker is authorized to engage any other broker or agent in connection with this Agreement, and Broker agrees to cooperate with other brokers or agents in endeavoring to obtain offers for the lease of the Property. Notwithstanding the involvement of a broker or agent cooperating with or claiming under Broker (a "Cooperating Broker"), the amount of the commission to be paid by Owner represents the full amount Owner is obligated to pay to Broker. Owner has no obligation or liability for the payment of any commission or fee to any Cooperating Broker without a written agreement by Owner to the contrary. Owner shall not enter into any agreement for the payment of a commission to a Cooperating Broker (for which Broker would be responsible) without the prior written consent of Broker.

7. <u>Duties</u>. Broker will use reasonable efforts to diligently seek offers from bona fide third party prospects for the lease of the Property. Signs and marketing materials will be prepared by Broker. Broker will market the Property online and use resources it deems appropriate to make the Property know to potential Lessees.

8. <u>Owner's Agreements</u>. Owner agrees to: (a) immediately refer to Broker all inquiries, offers and other indications of interest concerning the Property and to conduct all negotiations with prospective tenants through Broker; (b) make available to Broker all data, records and documents pertaining to the Property and to allow Broker to show the Property at reasonable times, and (c) authorize Broker to enter upon the Property for the purpose to show the Property and perform other activity to promote the leasing of the Property.

9. <u>Severability</u>. Any provision of this Agreement that is determined to be invalid or unenforceable under applicable law shall, to the extent possible without invalidating the remaining provisions, be construed or applied in such manner as will permit enforcement.

10. <u>Governing Law</u>. This Agreement shall be governed by and construed in accordance with the laws of the State of _____.

11. <u>Time of Essence</u>. Time is of the essence under this Agreement.

12. <u>Assignment</u>. This Agreement is a personal services contract; Broker shall not assign its rights or obligations under this Agreement without the prior written consent of Owner, not to be unreasonably withheld.

13. <u>Entire Agreement; Amendment</u>. This Agreement (including all exhibits and documents referred to in it) represents the entire agreement between the parties concerning the subject matter of this Agreement, and supersedes all prior agreements and arrangements as to such subject matter. This Agreement may not be amended or modified except in writing signed by the parties.

14. <u>Independent Contractor</u>. Broker is an independent contractor and will not be deemed an employee, agent, joint venturer or partner of Owner.

15. _Exculpation; Mutual Indemnification_. Notwithstanding anything herein to the contrary, Broker and Owner agree that the Owner, Broker, their respective shareholders, members, managers, directors, officers, employees and agents and any of their personal assets shall not be liable hereunder. The parties each mutually agree to indemnify and hold the other harmless from and against any loss, claim, demand, liability, cause of action, expense or cost arising by virtue of or attributable to the acts or omissions of Broker or Owner as the case may be, its agents or employees (including, but not limited to, any misrepresentation made by either party, its agents or employees to any third party)

16. _Successors and Assigns_. This Agreement shall be binding upon and shall inure to the benefit of the parties hereto and their permitted successors and assigns.

17. _Benefit_. This Agreement is solely for the benefit of the Owner and the Broker. No other person shall be deemed a third party beneficiary of this Agreement.

18. _Attorneys' Fees_. If either party brings any action to enforce its rights under this Agreement, the prevailing party is entitled to recover its reasonable attorney's fees and costs in connection with such action.

19. _Notices_. Any notice, or other communication required or permitted under this Agreement will be deemed effectively given when hand delivered, mailed by certified mail, or sent by nationally recognized courier (in each instance, prepaid) or sent via email, with proper addresses indicated below (or as may be changed by notice given in accordance with this Section):

To Broker: _____
_____
_____

To Owner: _____
_____
_____

20. <u>Counterparts; Execution.</u> This Agreement may be signed in any number of counterparts. Electronic or facsimile execution is binding for all purposes.

BROKER HEREBY NOTIFIES OWNER THAT BROKER WILL NOT DISCRIMINATE AGAINST ANY POTENTIAL PURCHASER OR TENANT ON THE BASIS OF RACE, COLOR, RELIGION, SEX, NATIONAL ORIGIN, ANCESTRY, PHYSICAL DISABILITY OR MARITAL STATUS. BROKER AGREES TO HOLD OWNER, ITS AGENTS, SUCCESSORS AND ASSIGNEES HARMLESS FROM ANY LIABILITY, DAMAGES, COSTS, ATTORNEY'S FEES, OR EXPENSES WHATSOEVER, ARISING FROM ANY AND ALL DISCRIMINATORY ACTIONS BY BROKER.

IN WITNESS WHEREOF, the parties hereto have executed this Agreement as of the Effective Date.

BROKER:

By: _____

Name: _____

Title: _____

OWNER:

By: _____

Name: _____

Title: _____

Form 2

EXCLUSIVE LISTING AGREEMENT
(Lease)

THIS EXCLUSIVE LISTING AGREEMENT ("Agreement") is made and entered into, by and between _____ whose address is _____ ("Owner"), and _____ _____ ("Broker"), whose address is _____ and is dated as of _____.

Recitals

A. Owner desires to appoint Broker as its sole and exclusive agent to lease the Real Estate as defined below; and

B. Broker is willing to accept the appointment as sole and exclusive agent under the terms of this Agreement.

NOW, THEREFORE, in consideration of the mutual covenants and agreements set forth herein, the parties agree as follows:

1. **Listing and Term.** Broker shall seek tenant(s) for the real property known as: _____, together with its improvements (collectively, the "Real Estate"), also identified as parcel_____ in _____. Owner grants Broker the exclusive right to lease for a period commencing on the full execution hereof and ending on _____ ("Exclusive Period"). The lease rate for the Real Estate is as set forth in the attached Schedule 1. All lease negotiations shall be conducted by Owner and any lease agreement shall be subject to the final review and approval by Owner in Owner's sole discretion. Owner shall have no obligation to enter into any lease agreement.
2. **Protection Period.** If the Real Estate is leased within _____days after the expiration or termination of this Agreement to anyone procured through the efforts of the Broker or to whom Broker showed the Real Estate during the Term, then this

Agreement will be extended to coincide with the execution date of the lease ("Protection Period").

3. **Broker's Commission.** If the Real Estate is leased the commission ("Commission") will be computed in accordance with the attached Schedule 2 "Schedule of Fees." Commission is deemed earned and is due and payable upon execution of a lease regardless of the Tenant's credit or future performance under the Lease. Execution and delivery of a lease to anyone to whom the Real Estate was shown during Exclusive Period entitles Broker to commission(s) as stated in this Agreement. Any portion of Commission not paid to Broker when due will bear interest from the due date until paid at the lesser of _____ (_____ %) per annum or the maximum legal rate of interest. Owner acknowledges that Broker has the right to utilize the state Commercial Broker Lien Law regarding earned commission, provided that the state has Broker lien rights.

4. **Alternative Transaction.** During the term of this Agreement and the Protection Period, if a proposed transaction occurs that is not specifically covered by this Agreement, including, without limitation, an exchange, build-to-suit, option to purchase, right of first refusal, ground lease, lease purchase, sale of stock or interests, sale of the mortgage note, or outright purchase and sale, then Broker automatically, without any further act by Owner or Broker, and without an amendment to this Agreement, is entitled to a Commission on such transaction under this Agreement. If the Real Estate is exchanged, the Commission will be computed on the fair market value of the Real Estate and is deemed earned and payable upon consummation of the transaction.

5. **Earnest Money Deposit.** Broker is authorized, but is not obligated, to act as a trust agent to accept and deposit in a non-interest bearing trust account upon acceptance of offers, earnest money or security deposits from prospective tenants making written offers to lease the Real Estate. At Closing, Broker may apply as much of the earnest money or security deposit as may be necessary to pay the applicable Commission. If any contract to lease does not close for any reason other than as agreed, the deposit shall be held by Broker, or other trust agent, until Owner, tenant and Broker mutually agree in writing to its disposition or until disposition is directed by a court of competent jurisdiction.

6. **Prospects.** Owner will refer to Broker all inquiries made by prospects or by brokers who contact Owner concerning the Real Estate and will send Broker the names and contact information of such prospects or brokers. Any lease of the Real Estate made to any such prospect or through such broker during the Exclusive Period, or within the Protection Period, is governed by this Agreement.

7. **Signage.** Broker, at ☐ Broker's sole cost and expense/ ☐ Owner's sole cost and expense, ☐ 50/50 shared between Owner and Broker is granted the exclusive right to place one or more "AVAILABLE" or "FOR LEASE" signs on the Real Estate during the Exclusive Period subject to applicable laws. Within _____ (_____) days after the termination or expiration of this Agreement, Broker will remove all signs it placed at the Real Estate. Broker is granted the right to market the property online using all resources it deems appropriate.

8. **Broker Cooperation.** Broker will cooperate with other brokers and their agents ("Tenant Broker(s)") to procure a tenant. Broker is authorized to offer compensation to Tenant Brokers provided Tenant Broker makes the initial submission of the Real Estate and conducts the introduction of the Tenant. It is Broker's policy to cooperate with other brokerages on an equal and consistent basis. Broker and its agents will make this listing available to Tenant Brokers to show, provide information that is not confidential, and present all offers submitted by other brokerages in a timely and objective manner.

9. **Fees and Expenses.** Marketing costs, including online marketing, are the responsibility of ☐ Broker ☐ Owner or ☐ _____. These costs will include, but not be limited to out-of-pocket expenses incurred by Broker pertaining to the marketing of the Real Estate, airfare, meals, transportation and all costs incurred in the preparation and distribution of marketing materials (e.g., photography, cartography, graphic arts, reproductions, printing, etc.). All marketing materials ☐ are ☐ are not subject to Owner's prior approval.

10. **Broker's Services.**

a) <u>Licensed Real Estate Broker.</u> Broker represents and warrants to Owner that it holds a valid real estate broker's license issued by the State of _____.

b) <u>Efforts.</u> Broker will make an earnest, continuous effort to lease the Real Estate under the terms and conditions of this Agreement. Broker will undertake to identify prospective tenants through an aggressive canvassing campaign. Broker will seek to contact potential tenants directly, to provide them clear and complete information on the Real Estate, and to follow up in a professional manner. Broker will actively and continuously solicit the cooperation of all commercial-industrial real estate agents in the primary and secondary marketing areas using, as appropriate personal letter, brochure, and email. Broker will employ high ethical standards and professionalism at all times.

c) <u>Reporting.</u> Broker agrees to inform Owner promptly of all offers and inquiries with respect to the Real Estate. Owner will promptly refer all inquiries received during the Exclusive Period to Broker. Broker shall meet (in person or by phone) with Owner, and provide such information and documentation relating to Broker's efforts hereunder, as reasonably requested by Owner from time to time.

d) <u>Disclosure.</u> Neither Broker nor any employee or agent of Broker shall make any representations or warranties regarding the Real Estate. Owner will make available to Broker the documents and other information which, in the reasonable judgment of Owner and Broker, are necessary or appropriate for the fulfilment of Broker's assignment hereunder and the proper marketing of the Real Estate. All such information shall be supplied without representation or warranty.

e) <u>Return of Materials.</u> Upon completion of a successful lease transaction or upon the termination or expiration of this Agreement, Broker will return to Owner on or before thirty (30) days following the termination or expiration date: all keys, property, supplies, contracts, books and records furnished by Owner, drawings, reports and correspondence in Broker's possession at the time of termination or expiration of this Agreement and all other papers or documents pertaining to the Real Estate which are the property of

Owner. Broker is allowed to retain originals or copies of books and records as required to comply with applicable law.

f) <u>Property Management.</u> Broker does not assume nor is it charged with responsibility for the custody, management, care, maintenance, protection, or repair of the Real Estate nor for the protection or custody of any personal property located thereon, unless otherwise provided by separate written agreement.

11. **<u>Representation of Authority.</u>** Owner represents that it is the owner of the Real Estate and/or has the full right, power and authority to execute this Agreement and to consummate a transaction as provided herein. The person signing below on behalf of Broker represents that the signer has the authority to enter into this Agreement on behalf of Broker.

12. **<u>Showings.</u>** Owner authorizes Broker to conduct key-entry showings of the Real Estate during the term of this Agreement. Owner represents that adequate insurance will be kept in force to protect Owner in the event of any damage, losses or claims arising from entry to the Real Estate under this Agreement and hereby holds harmless Broker, its agents and employees, from any loss, claim or damage resulting there from.

13. **<u>Indemnity.</u>** Owner acknowledges that Broker is relying on all information provided herein or supplied by Owner or Owner's sources and/or Tenant or Tenant's sources in connection with the Real Estate. Owner agrees to indemnify, hold harmless and defend Broker, its agents and employees, from any claims, demands, damages, suits, liabilities, costs and expenses (including reasonable attorney's fees) arising out of (a) any misrepresentation or concealment of facts by Owner or Owner's sources and/or Tenant or Tenant's sources, or (b) any condition, event, accident, or injury related to any entry onto the Real Estate, whether by Broker or any third party, it being understood that Broker shall have no liability or cost of any kind related to a showing or other event on or about the Real Estate.

14. **<u>Publicity.</u>** Owner consents to Broker publicizing its role in any completed transaction.

15. **Survival.** This Agreement is binding upon the parties hereto and their respective successors and assigns. The terms "Broker", "Owner", "Tenant", and/or "Buyer" shall include affiliates, successors, assigns and nominees.

16. **Counterparts.** This Agreement may be executed in two or more counterparts, all of which shall be considered one and the same agreement. A facsimile or electronic signature is fully binding on the parties

17. **Applicable State and Federal Laws.** The parties hereto agree to comply with all applicable federal, state and local laws, regulations, codes, ordinances and administrative orders having jurisdiction over the parties, the Real Estate or the subject matter of this Agreement, including, but not limited to, the 1964 Civil Rights Act and all amendments thereto, the Foreign Investment In Real Property Tax Act, the Comprehensive Environmental Response Compensation and Liability Act, and the Americans with Disabilities Act.

18. **Taxes.** Should there be any tax, fee, or other cost leveed in regard to the property due Broker, such tax, fee, or other cost shall be paid by Owner. Nothing herein requires Owner to pay an income tax or earnings tax.

19. **Entire Agreement.** This Agreement is a legal and binding contract between all parties including their heirs, representatives, successors and assigns. This Agreement constitutes the entire agreement between the parties concerning the matters set out in it, and no oral or implied agreement, representation or understanding shall cancel or vary the terms of this Agreement. Owner acknowledges that Owner has read and received a completed copy of this Agreement and attachments and the information contained herein is true and accurate to the best of Owner's knowledge.

ACCEPTED BY:

BROKER: _____

By: _____
Date: _____
Name: _____
Title: _____

OWNER: _____

By: _____
Date: _____
Name: _____
Title: _____

SCHEDULE 1
SCHEDULE OF LEASE TRANSACTION TERMS

1) **Rent.** Annual rent, payable monthly in advance, shall be:

   ($_____ **MONTHLY OR** $_____- **/SF ANNUALLY**)

   net of building operating expenses or as otherwise negotiated by _____ and accepted by Owner.

2) **Lease Term.** The term of lease shall be for _____ months or longer.

3) **Expense Reimbursement Items.** Tenant shall pay, as reimbursement to Owner, its pro-rata share of increases to the following operating expenses: real estate taxes and assessments and any increases thereof, "all-risk" insurance on the real estate and improvements thereon and any increases thereof, common area maintenance (CAM), gas, electric, water, sewer, house electric, exterior grounds keeping, trash pickup, and janitorial service. Current reimbursable items total:

casualty insurance	$_____
real estate taxes	$_____
CAM	$_____
total expenses	$_____

4) **Tenant Expenses.** Tenant shall pay for its own account the following expenses: _____

5) **Tenant Maintenance.** Tenant, at its expense, shall be responsible for the maintenance and repair of the following items: _____.

6) **Owner Maintenance.** _____ shall be responsible for the roof, structure, replacement of capital components, and the cost and administration of grounds keeping and exterior maintenance.

SCHEDULE 2
SCHEDULE OF LEASE FEES

Lease Commission. In consideration of Broker's effort and service to procure a Tenant for the Real Estate, Owner agrees to pay Broker a Commission of _____ percent (___%) of the aggregate base rent for which the Real Estate may be leased regardless of agency relationships. Should any renewal or expansion occur, the Owner agrees to pay Broker a Commission of _____ percent (____ %) of the aggregate rent under said renewal or expansion, payable at the commencement of each new term. If the Tenant procured by Broker purchases the Real Estate, or any part thereof, during the term of the lease, including renewals, Owner agrees to pay Broker a sale Commission of _____ percent (____ %) of the sale price less any unearned lease Commission. Owner agrees to incorporate Broker's entitlement to fees into the lease document. If a Tenant Broker introduces the Tenant to the property, and the Tenant successfully enters into a binding lease of the Real Estate, Broker shall compensate the Tenant Broker out of the total fee paid to Broker

MARKETING MANAGEMENT

Marketing strategy has developed in quantum leaps with the advent of the Internet, social media, and a rapidly increasing array of high-tech tools. There are mountains of resources and tons of qualified specialists who can increase your credibility in the marketplace.

For purposes of this volume, we believe we can be of help by gently reminding you of the different dimensions of marketing property for lease. We also point out how each property fits into the long range goal of improving your own profile and status of the firm you work for. Please note that some suggestions here will require the participation of your company. Try to develop a good relationship with the marketing team in your firm. Be willing to defend expenditures you request and make an effort to provide as much measurable information as possible to prove the value of a marketing spend.

General Ideas

Because the Marketing Management Plan is primarily targeted to a single property, we believe it is helpful to stress the areas you must explore for long term career with company building success. Think about the following activities in the context of improving your ability to obtain listings and make yourself a "go-to" professional in the community:

1. Build and maintain a personal "brand"[3]
2. Do what you can to optimize the company website/app;
3. Develop search engine optimization (SEO). Work with a professional to make your targeted visibility pop;
4. Use social media resources to build awareness of you and your firm;

---

[3] Note – Be careful to accomplish this in the context of your brokerage firm's identity. Do not violate company guidelines. Hopefully your firm will have a marketing person who will assist you in this endeavor. Never forget you are a part of a team, but also don't settle for being a mere part of the woodwork.

5. Become a face in the world you work in through attendance at meetings, events, and community service;
6. Develop relationships with the people you deal with through professional, respectful, and honest dealings;
7. Make an effort to be in the press. Make friends with journalists and media folks;
8. Work with a top-notch promotional firm to keep your identity and brand in sight as much as possible;
9. Advertise as appropriate in the right places; and
10. Refine your strategy. Measure, measure and remeasure to be sure you receive a good return on your money. Focus on an optimum return on the marketing budget.

The following, as included, can be used to plan and implement a leasing property marketing strategy.

Tip:

Develop a Hook. Maybe you are the guy who always has a new joke or the one who knows more about professional soccer than anyone else. Everyone can develop, refine and highlight some special personal trait that helps promote being memorable. Be remembered not forgotten.

Leasing Management Plan

		Budgeted	Designed	Completed	Approval
1.	Post the Property Online				
	a. Costar				
	b. LoopNet				
	c. Company Website				
2.	Print Media				
	a. Brochure				
	b. Mailer				
3.	Sign(s)				
4.	Individual Property Website				
5.	Virtual Reality Tour(s)				
6.	E-mail Campaign				
7.	Social Media Campaign				
	a. Twitter				
	b. LinkedIn				
	c. Facebook				
	d. Instagram				
8.	Open House				
9.	Special Promotion				
	a. "Gift" for Appropriate Lease to Brokers				
	b. Extra Commission/Spread to Tenant Brokers				
10.	Enlist Interested Third Parties				
	a. Local Development Attorney				

b. Chamber of Commerce				
c. Other				
11. Press Campaign				
a. Place articles				
b. Outreach to journalists				
12. Print/Billboard/Nontraditional Advertising				
13. Creative Showings				
a. Bus Tour				
b. Limousine Tour				
c. Other				

INTRODUCTION TO PRE-LEASE REIMBURSEMENT LETTER AGREEMENT

The attached is offered as a possible solution to a problem which sometimes arises in the negotiation of a lease. Often the deal does not move forward in a perfectly synchronized form. To get the deal done requires monetary commitment before the lease is finished.

This form works to bridge the gap between the executed lease and the negotiation phase. If the Landlord does not want to be left holding a bag of expenses while the Tenant walks free, it may suggest a letter agreement like this. If a Tenant wants to demonstrate its good faith and commitment and needs to get a Landlord involved it may suggest this type of arrangement. The Landlord who may otherwise fear it is being "shopped" may be more willing to hire a lawyer and /or space planner if it has an agreement for reimbursement in hand.

This particular letter is set up to outline terms and is written by Landlord to Tenant. Naturally, with appropriate changes this form can be revised so that it comes from the Tenant to the Landlord.

Do not provide this to any third party until the protocol has been approved by your attorney.

Pre-Lease Reimbursement Letter Agreement

_____, 20___

  RE: _____

      _____
("Prospective Landlord")

      _____
("Prospective Tenant" or you)

      _____
("Leased Premises")

  Dear _____:

  This letter, when signed by you as Prospective Tenant will form an agreement between you and Prospective Landlord dealing with certain preliminary costs in connection with a possible lease ("Lease") of the Premises to you. Although this is binding for the limited purpose of assuring Prospective Landlord that it will be paid certain amounts, this letter shall not be construed as a lease, offer or option to lease, or an enforceable reservation of space. Neither party is bound to lease any space to or from the other until a Lease is fully executed and delivered. The following outlines terms pursuant to which activities will be taken before the Lease is consummated:

    _____ Landlord drafting Lease
    _____ Landlord obtaining space plans/designs/drawings
    _____ Landlord processing approvals
    _____ Other: _____

  As consideration for the items checked above, Prospective Tenant agrees that if Prospective Landlord incurs cost for those items, but Prospective Tenant fails to sign the Lease for any reason within ____ (___) days after the Lease is submitted to Prospective Tenant or if a Lease is not executed for any reason/no reason, then Prospective Tenant will reimburse Landlord for all fees and expenses paid or incurred by Prospective Landlord to carry out of the work checked above, subject to a cap on Prospective Tenant's obligations of $_____. In order for Prospective Landlord to go forward you will pre-pay $_____ towards the above described expense. If the Lease is fully executed and delivered, the pre-paid amount will be applied to Prospective Tenant's payment obligations due on execution.

Please confirm your acceptance by returning a signed copy of this letter agreement to us and by making arrangements for the pre-payment to be made to us at that time. A fax, PDF or electronic signature is fully binding for all purposes.

Very truly yours,

By: _____
Title: _____
Name: _____

ACCEPTED AND AGREED TO this ____ day of _____, 20___.
_____

By: _____
    Authorized Signer

Print Name: _____

Title: _____

INTRODUCTION TO LEASE NEGOTIATIONS

There are many approaches to getting a lease negotiation completed. Many landlords develop what amounts to a standard form of proposal which contains the essential parts of the deal. We have provided a sample Proposal Form for your review. Note that the form has a specific reference to the need for tenant financials. This is a very important item that many Brokers do not fully appreciate. Landlords do not want to get burned by tenants who turn out to be short-lived or constantly in default. When you represent the landlord, think of the economics. Most deals require landlord to absorb:

1. Cost of Buildout (Tenant Improvement Costs)

2. Cost of Lease Preparation and Design (Legal/Design Costs)

3. Brokerage Expense

If the deal goes bad early in the lease term, the landlord's economics are lousy. Just as an example, suppose the landlord spends $92,000.00 on buildout and tenant improvements (most of which are specialized and thus not useable in future deals) for a small restaurant space; pays $8,000.00 for expenses and legal fees; pays commission on $20,000.00. Suppose there are two months free rent and the tenant tanks in month seven after two months of unpaid rent. Even if some bankruptcy recovery is successful, the landlord is probably out over $100,000.00. Even in the unlikely event that improvements are good for the next tenant, this is a bad result. And if the next tenant is a dance studio, then the restaurant work is largely useless.

Some landlords use a letter of intent (LOI) which is similar to the proposal, but often more detailed. Some Brokers/landlords prefer the more formal nature of a LOI, others feel it may be best to use closer to the end of the process. We are attaching an example of a LOI which can be adjusted to meet the circumstances of a particular deal.

A caveat about letters of intent or signed proposals should be added. Even with clear language stating that the letter is <u>not</u> binding, there are court decisions that have held that the letter can be binding or that the letter creates a duty to negotiate in good faith.

Thus, some attorneys discourage the use of letters of intent. Even if the document does not create a binding agreement, the imposition of a duty to negotiate in good faith puts a special limitation on the ability to fully explore all options and to use appropriate negotiating tactics.

One other approach is to circulate a term sheet which contains the same content, but is not signed.

Overall, whether you use a term sheet, proposal, or LOI there are enough issues and questions that we urge that the Broker encourage clients to have counsel review the documents and be a part of the process early in the game.

Lease Proposal Form

PROPOSAL FOR OFFICE SPACE

DATE OF PROPOSAL: _____

TENANT: _____

LANDLORD: _____

BUILDING: _____

PREMISES: _____

USE: _____

RENTABLE SQUARE FEET: _____

LEASE TERM: _____

RENEWAL TERM: _____

LEASE COMMENCEMENT: _____

BASE RENTAL RATE: $_____
                                ANNUAL: $_____
                                MONTHLY $_____

BASE RENT ESCALATION: ____% per Year

ADDITIONAL RENT
(REAL ESTATE TAXES
& OPERATING EXPENSES):   Tenant is responsible for proportionate share of Real Estate Taxes and Operating Expenses.

For illustration purposes:

The current aggregate Tax and Operating Expense is _____/rentable square foot and current annual expense is $_____ (_____/month).

CAP: Tenant will have a __% per year cap on controllable expenses calculated on a cumulative basis.

RENT ABATEMENT: Landlord will abate Base Rent for the following months:

TENANT IMPROVEMENTS ALLOWANCE: Landlord shall provide an improvement allowance in the amount of $_____ to be used only for building improvements.

BROKERS: Landlord's broker is _____. Tenant's broker is _____. Landlord shall pay commission by other separate written agreement.

FINANCIALS: THE TERMS AND CONDITIONS OUTLINED IN THIS PROPOSAL ARE CONTINGENT ON LANDLORD'S REVIEW OF TENANT'S FINANCIAL CONDITION. Landlord reserves the right to require a guaranty of lease, cash security deposit or other security deposits. Tenant shall submit to Landlord two full years of financial statements plus a completed credit application and credit authorization form.

NOT BINDING: This proposal does not constitute a contract between the parties; it is not intended to be binding on either party. This proposal is merely for the parties to seek to outline of terms and to negotiate a formal and binding agreement. In no event shall either party incur any liability if it fails to execute a formal and binding agreement.

Landlord may be presenting proposals to others and it reserves the right to accept any other proposal or to withdraw from negotiations at any time.

This proposal is open until _____. If acceptable, please sign below and return via email. On receipt, Landlord will prepare a lease agreement.

Sincerely,

_____

Agreed and Accepted by:

Name: _____

Signature: _____

Date: _____

Letter of Intent

[FIRM NAME]

_____ __, 20____

_____
_____
_____

RE: LOI - _____ ("Property")

Dear _____:

The purpose of this letter is to outline basic terms with respect to the lease of space in the facility located at _____. The basic terms and conditions of the proposed lease are as follows:

Tenant: _____

Landlord: _____

Use: _____

Premises: _____

Lease Term: _____ months

Options: Tenant shall have _____ renewal options of _____ each upon no less than _____ days advance written notice before the term ends.

Free Rent: _____ months.

Base Rent: _____
Renewal rent will continue on same terms with _____ annual increases.

Taxes, Common Area, Maintenance, Insurance: _____

Security Deposit: _____

Utilities: Tenant will pay all utility costs directly to the respective utility company. Tenant is responsible for its pro-rata share of water and sewer charges.

Tenant Improvement Allowance: Landlord will provide a Tenant Improvement Allowance of $_____.

Condition of Premises: Landlord will turn the space over to Tenant in AS IS condition; all building systems (sprinklers, plumbing, electrical, etc.) will be in good working order and code compliant.

Repair and Maintenance: Landlord shall keep the structural portions of the Premises in good order and condition. Tenant is responsible for all non-structural repairs, maintenance and replacements.

Assignment/Subletting: Tenant shall not assign, sublet, transfer, or encumber the lease without written consent of Landlord. Landlord's consent will not be unreasonably withheld, conditioned or delayed. No consent needed for corporate transfer/merger/etc.

Identification/Signage: Tenant, at its sole cost and expense, shall provide interior and exterior identification. The design and location of said identification to be subject to Landlord's prior approval, which shall not be unreasonably withheld or delayed and will comply with all governmental regulations.

Delivery Date:	Landlord shall deliver the space upon full execution of the lease and completion of any Landlord Work.
Lease Commencement:	The lease shall commence upon delivery of the Premises from Landlord to Tenant.
Rent Commencement:	Rent shall commence at the earlier of _____ days after lease commencement or Tenant's opening for business.
Landlord Contingency:	This lease proposal is contingent upon approval of Tenant and Guarantor financial statements which shall by submitted for review by Landlord.
Guaranty:	The lease shall be guaranteed by _____.
Brokerage:	Landlord shall pay a commission to _____ and _____ (pursuant to a separate agreement).

    The purpose of this letter is only to outline the major terms under which the parties intend to proceed for negotiation of a lease on the Premises. It does not create any duty to negotiate in good faith. It is not a binding document. A binding agreement shall not be deemed to be made until such time as a mutually acceptable lease has been fully executed and all contingencies have been removed from that lease.

    If the above is acceptable please sign below and forward to me at _____. Email, facsimile, or electronic execution is fully acceptable. Further, it is understood that until this is fully accepted, Landlord reserves the right to negotiate with and market proposals to, others. Nothing herein will prevent either party from withdrawing from negotiations at any time.

_____

Approved and accepted this _____ day of _____, 20____.

By: _____
Title: _____

SECTION III: REPRESENTING THE TENANT

"The supreme quality for leadership is unquestionably integrity. Without it, no real success is possible, no matter whether it is on a section gang, a football field, in an army, or in an office."

~ Dwight D. Eisenhower

INTRODUCTION TO REPRESENTING THE TENANT

It will help to step back and review the role played by a Broker representing the Tenant. The expectations of the various people involved in a particular transaction may lead each to wear a particular set of blinders. In the end, the Broker may be treated like a ping pong ball—batted back and forth. By focusing on the key elements of the deal the Broker can best serve the client and facilitate not just one lease, but act to build a foundation for a successful career.

I.   Fiduciary Role

First, the Broker must never lose sight that he or she acts as a fiduciary for the client. This is not merely a legal concept – and surely this is stapled on Broker's forehead by licensing classes, continuing education and company practices and procedures – but it also helps focus on how much must be done to guard and serve the client. You have a special relationship and a special set of duties. Serving those obligations faithfully will build a sound reputation, pay off for the client and avoid damaging claims and sanctions.

The Broker must learn what the client needs. Thus, the Broker must put together a template by listening and asking the right questions. By building the parameters for the suitable location and terms, the Broker will be able to better serve the client and will save time and effort.

II. Understanding the Market

The Broker's toolbox also needs to contain not only the information unique to the client, but that which covers the market. Sound knowledge of what is going on in local demographics, politics and economics will help. By being an informed member of the community, the Broker learns to see where the best bargains are and what is hot and what is not. If housing is growing in the West and the client needs rooftops, then look West.

Locating property is further augmented by good organizational and technological tools. Programs which provide geographic searching are of great help. Knowing that a particular entity may be looking to downsize and sublet and knowing when and how to contact the decision-maker is of great help too.

Once the site or sites are found, then the Broker must again pull out the organizational/commercial skillset and present these locations to the client. If the identified locations are a bust – back to the drawing board. It is a process which constantly requires shifting of focus and reexamination.

III. <u>Assistance with Negotiations</u>

If the site is set and approved, the Broker will often be called to assist in the negotiation process. The Broker's knowledge will be critical because he/she can apply market knowledge and experience to real issues. Is the landlord's rental rate realistic? Will the landlord give free rent? Does the property need another tenant in place to attract a sale?

A. <u>Be Creative</u>

Here is an area where creativity can be invaluable. Suppose the Broker knows that a new building will be constructed soon just up the road from the target site. The new building owner will make a sweetheart deal with your client, but the new property won't be available for at least three years. By knowing this, the Broker can work for a lease which includes a right to terminate early after the second lease year. Then, when the new building is up, the tenant can take advantage of the opportunity.

B. <u>Assemble a Team</u>

As pointed out above, during the negotiation process the Broker can further assist the client by having assembled a team that can obtain the best results. Broker can use his experience to recruit good architects, attorneys, accountants, environmental consultants, title companies etc. The team approach can be invaluable. If the site has environmental issues and the Broker knows an environmental consultant who is quick and reasonable and who can confirm that the building is acceptable for client without building a career out of the situation, then the Broker has given its client good service.

Also, try to give more than one recommendation so that the client has the opportunity to obtain a second option/opinion. The

A strong team will tend to reduce the stresses on the client and minimize expenses. If your referrals are professional with lots of experience, they will know what is important and concentrate on that.

C. Assess Expertise and Personalities

Expertise and sensitivity to personality types are essential tools for you in the negotiation stage. Is the landlord's counsel inexperienced because he/she does mostly bankruptcy work? Let your client's attorney know. Has the landlord suffered bad economic circumstances for years and therefore, needs the deal to get a loan? Advise the client and his attorney. Simply put, a good agent constantly listens and pays attention.

IV. Be Professional

Completion of a lease also requires the Broker to be willing to advise and communicate. Depending on the particular personalities the Broker's role will vary. Some lawyers are very adverse to feedback – but if the Broker can set the terms, define deal parts and provide insight, the client may benefit. If you see a mistake, share the knowledge. But do it respectfully. Don't knowingly embarrass professionals by raising questions in a way that suggests they are not doing a good job. Sometimes for strategic reasons, counsel will choose to fight certain issues, but not others. Check with them offline when possible in order to preserve a good working relationship and avoid to appearing to be either a know-it-all or an ignoramus.

INTRODUCTION TO THE DUE DILIGENCE CHECKLIST

One of the roles of the Broker representing the Tenant can involve participation in the Due Diligence process. This process can be monumental in scope or can be largely ignored - - it all depends on the Tenant, the size of the deal, and the circumstances. Here is a Due Diligence checklist which can be used to organize the items that may need to be handled and to assign responsibility for management of those items.

Tip:

See the Big Picture. Make sure you understand the client's goals. One retailer provided a form lease which was fabulously fair, indeed clearly landlord friendly. The first reaction was to suggest revising to "WIN" more points. Digging into the retailer's true goals prevented a lot of grief. This particular business housed in standalone buildings wanted to be able to get excellent cap on its leases. By accepting more lease responsibilities and drafting documents free of "gotchas", this company made landlords hungry for its product, driving down cap rates and making it a popular product.

Due Diligence Checklist

		Date Requested	Received	Status	Responsible Party
I.	**GOVERNMENTAL/GENERAL/POLITICAL**				
A.	Political situation				
B.	Fees and taxes				
C.	Any abatements or incentives				
II.	**MARKET INFORMATION**				
A.	Comparable rent information				
B.	Market report and vacancy data				
C.	Incentives				
III.	**PROPERTY INFORMATION**				
A.	Location and area				
	1. Address				
	2. City				
	3. Building type				
	4. Building size				
	5. Access details				
	6. Traffic details				
	7. Parking details				
B.	Property condition report				
	1. Interior common area				
	2. Exterior common area				
	3. Proposed premises				

	Date Requested	Received	Status	Responsible Party
C. Cost estimates				
1. Deferred maintenance				
2. Improvements				
3. Overall budget				
D. Site plan/survey				
E. Listing of personal property for space				
1. Any already on site?				
2. Needed?				
3. Cost estimates?				
F. Review warranties on:				
1. Roof				
2. HVAC equipment				
3. General contractor warranty				
4. Major subcontractor warranties				
5. Sprinkler				
6. Elevator				
7. Other				
G. Inspection reports				
1. Roof				
2. Structural systems				
3. Mechanical and electrical equipment				
4. Life safety systems				
5. Utility service				

			Date Requested	Received	Status	Responsible Party
		6. Parking lot				
		7. Elevators				
		8. ADA compliance				
		9. Other				
	H.	Insurance policies				
		1. Landlord policies				
		2. Required tenant coverage				
	I.	As-built plans and specs				
	J.	Certificates of occupancy				
	K.	Permits and licenses				
	L.	Preventative maintenance program				
IV.	**LEASE AND OPERATIONS**					
	A.	Standard form of lease				
	B.	Utility bills – last three (3) years				
	C.	Property tax bills for last three (3) years				
	D.	New tax bills				
	E.	Notices from tax authority				
	F.	Applicable service agreement/contracts summary				
V.	**LANDLORD INFORMATION**					
	A.	Entity status				
	B.	Current financial information				
	C.	Background information				

		Date Requested	Received	Status	Responsible Party
D.	Property management information				
E.	Landlord reputation				
F.	Lender/lender requirements				
VI. LEGAL					
A.	Lease Negotiation				
B.	Title (Title report)				
C.	Survey				
D.	CC&R's, easements, and common area agreements				
E.	ADA compliance				
VII. ENVIRONMENTAL					
A.	Review phase I (Phase II) environmental site assessment				
B.	New studies, if necessary				
C.	Soil sampling				
D.	Underground storage tanks				
E.	Groundwater sampling				
F.	Asbestos survey				
G.	Lead paint				
H.	Radon testing				
I.	Mold assessment				
J.	List of known hazardous material				
K.	Any issues from neighboring tenants? Properties?				

		Date Requested	Received	Status	Responsible Party
VIII.	**UTILITIES**				
	A. Water				
	B. Sewer				
	C. Gas				
	D. Electricity				
	E. Telephone				
	F. Internet				
	G. Drainage or other issues				
IX.	**LITIGATION**				
	A. Current/threatened actions against landlord?				
	B. Governmental actions/suits concerning the property?				
X.	**PERMITTING AND ZONING STATUS**				
	A. Zoning reports				
	B. Any planned zoning changes?				
	C. Fire alarm and life safety system certifications				
	D. Business licenses and applications, if any				
	E. Signage				
	F. Other				
XI.	**OTHER**				

INTRODUCTION TO TENANT QUALIFICATION

This form is an internal template for a Tenant representative. It is designed to capture important data to start the process and to make sure the work necessary to represent the potential lessee is worth the effort.

It can be used to:

1. Help determine the person(s) working in a particular brokerage office who are best suited for the representation.
2. Secure basic contact information.
3. Begin sorting out the best properties for the prospect.
4. Qualify the prospect to make sure it is an appropriate client for the brokerage.

Tenant Representation Qualification Form

BASIC INFORMATION	
Name	
Email	
Address	
Phone	
Fax	
NEEDS	
What kind of property do you require? (Flex, Industrial, Office, Retail, Other)	
Geographic Preference	
Annual Rent Budget	
Size of the Space	
Parking Requirements	
Special Needs	
Sprinklers	
Docks	
Drive-in	
Signage	
Storage	
Antennas/Communications	
Length of Term Desired	
Other	
What improvements do you anticipate? Describe anticipated costs and how improvements will be financed?	

BUSINESS DESCRIPTION	
How many years have you been in business?	
Current Business is Leased or Owned?	
If leased, please provide name and address of Landlord	
If owned, please provide the address	
Are you relocating?	
Are you interested in our assistance in marketing your current property?	
Why are you looking for space?	
Describe your business	
Describe your Business Experience	
What is the legal structure of your business? (Corporation, Partnership, LLC, Sole Proprietorship)	
If your business involves a franchise, please supply details	
FINANCIALS	
Current financial Statement (Please provide current financials and two years of tax returns. If this is a sole proprietorship or personally guaranteed lease, include personal information)	
Please provide bank reference	
Employer Identification	

Number (EIN)	
Indicate sources of income other than from above business (if applicable)	
MISC.	
How did you find out about us? (Referral, Advertising, Signs, Website, Direct Mail, Advertising, Other)	
Special issues or Questions?	

TENANT REPRESENTATION TRANSACTION MODEL

It helps for a Broker representing a tenant, especially a newer, less experienced Broker, to have a roadmap of the transaction from start to finish. This Transaction Model is an outline of the steps along the way, and can be adapted by a commercial Broker, as needed to, reflect her or his own process.

> **Tip:**
>
> ---
>
> **Return Calls and Reply to Emails.** You need not be compulsive, but you should be responsive. Even if you don't have the answer, let your client know that you are working on it. Even a simple "Got your email and will be in touch as soon as I have further information," goes a long way.

Tenant Representation Transaction Model

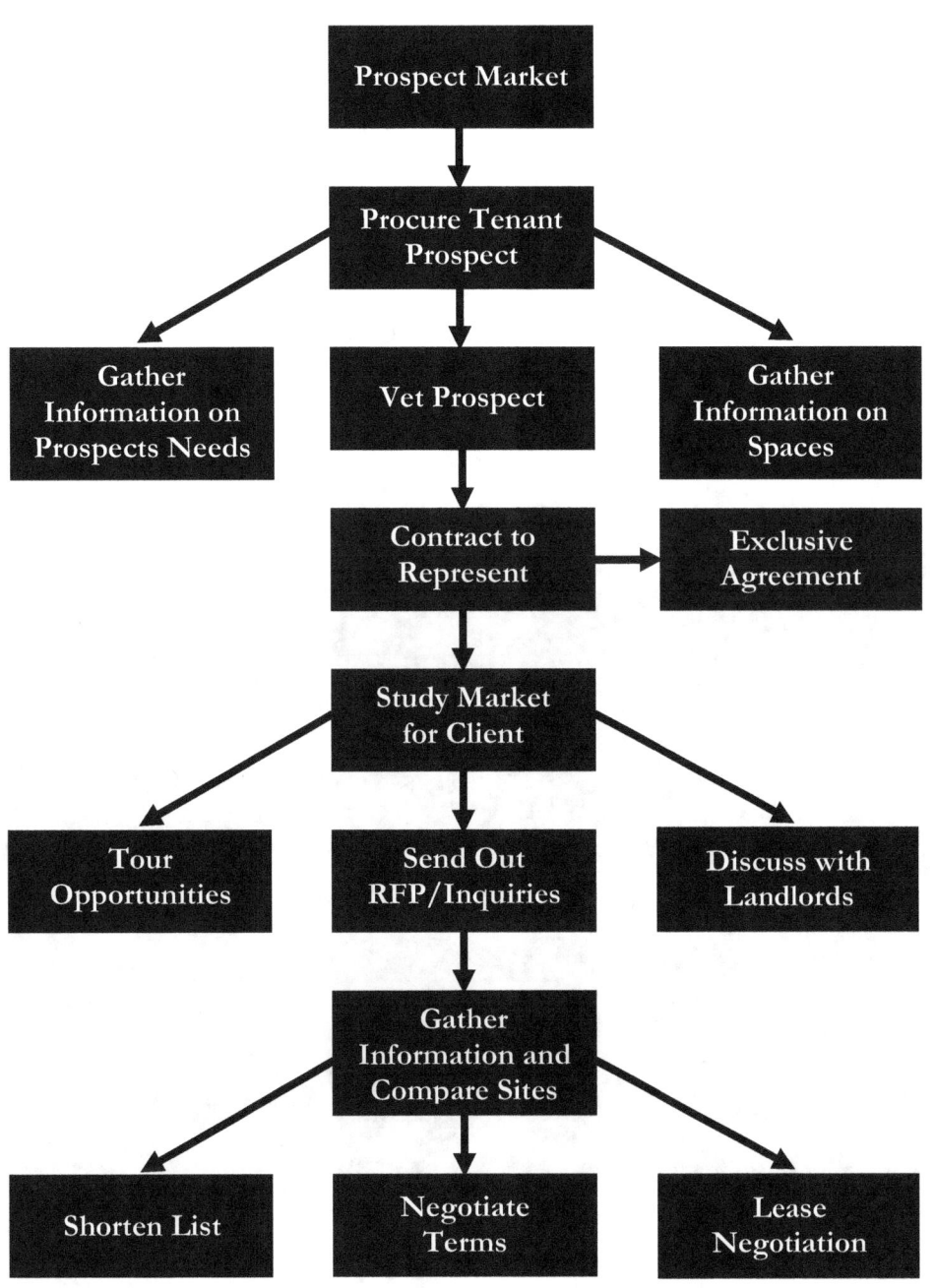

TENANT REPRESENTATIVE LETTER OF ENGAGEMENT AND REPRESENTATION

Sometimes tenants issue their own engagement letters, but more often than not, the Tenant's broker will be permitted to issue the controlling document. Here is an example of a representation agreement in the form of a letter agreement, to be submitted by the Broker and to be countersigned by the actual Tenant/Client. This form is fairly aggressive and takes several positions to which the Tenant may object. It calls for an attached schedule to define the payment of commission. Naturally this form should be reviewed by counsel before using.

Tenant Representative
Letter of Engagement and Representation

DATE

_____
_____
_____

RE: _____

Dear Client:

      This letter agreement ("Agreement") confirms your engagement of _____ (the "Broker" "we" or "us") to exclusively represent _____ ("Client", "Tenant", or "You") in seeking space ("Space) in the _____ market ("Market"). For good and valuable consideration which we mutually acknowledge, you agree that we will represent you subject to the following terms:

      1. The term starts on full execution of this Agreement and ends on_____, 20____. After that period, the term extends from month to month until terminated by either party on fifteen (15) days prior written notice.

      2. We will have the exclusive right to locate Space for your requirements and act as your real estate agent in the Market.

      3. We agree to use reasonable diligence in seeking to achieve the goals of this engagement and we are authorized to (a) select properties that substantially satisfy your criteria within the market, (b) present the selected opportunities to you, (c) assist you in evaluating and ranking the various alternatives, and (d) with your approval, negotiate a lease of Space. The decision whether to lease remains up to you.

4.   In the course of the transaction, if in our judgement we determine it appropriate to engage third party resources for items like plans, cost analysis, construction, etc., we will let you know. These engagements will be subject to your approval, and will be obtained at your sole cost.

5.   Landlord's agreement to pay our commission does not affect your duty to act exclusively through us.

6.   The owner of the Space shall pay Broker's commission in accordance with the attached commission schedule. If the owner does not agree to pay a commission acceptable to us, but a lease is consummated, Tenant shall be responsible for the balance of commission due us, so that we will receive our full commission. Further, should we fail to receive our full commission as a result of any Tenant default of any executed lease, we will be entitled to receive such shortage from the Tenant.

7.   If the property in which the Space is located or the Space itself is purchased by Tenant during the term of this agreement or during the term of the Lease or within 180 days after the Term or Lease ends, the Broker will be entitled to receive a commission of __% of the total sales price.

8.   For one (1) year after the expiration of this Agreement, you will designate us as the procuring broker in connection with any transaction submitted to you during the term of this Agreement for Space which you choose to lease. If, at the end of such period, lease/sale documents are out for signature, this Agreement will govern such transaction, but only if and when the transaction is completed.

9.   While Broker will act exclusively for you during the term of this Agreement, you acknowledge and agree that we may represent others with regard to the properties identified, shown or discussed with you during this Agreement.

10.   Notices under this Agreement are to be given in writing, by email, certified mail or recognized overnight delivery.

11. This Agreement (including any exhibits) constitutes our entire Agreement. Neither party will be bound by any representation except as expressly acknowledged in this Agreement, or by a written amendment to this signed by both parties. This Agreement will be governed by laws of the State of _____ and will be binding on the parties, their heirs successors, designees, and assigns.

12. If either party fails to comply with the terms of this Agreement the other party will have all rights and remedies at law and equity with respect to such default including, without limitation, the right to recover attorneys' fees and costs. In any proceeding concerning this Agreement or any transaction related to this Agreement, the prevailing party shall recover all reasonable costs and attorneys' fees from the other party.

13. You acknowledge that we are being retained solely as a real estate agent and not as an attorney, tax advisor, lender, engineer, or other professional. You are advised to seek professional advice concerning the condition of the space or concerning legal, tax matters, etc. Space shall be shown and made available to you without regard to race, color, religion, sex, handicap, familial status or national origin as well as classes protected by the laws of the United States, the State of _____, and applicable local jurisdictions.

14. Please confirm your agreement by having an authorized party sign and return the enclosed copy of this letter. Execution by PDF, facsimile or other digital means is fully binding.

_____

Agreed to:

_____

Dated: _____

NOTE: NEED TO ATTACH A COMMISSION SCHEDULE

RFP

The following is an example of a RFP form which can be used in a particular deal by a Tenant Representative. This form is deliberately comprehensive, mainly to give the prospective user the opportunity to select the general headings and provisions which it wishes to use and those it may want to stockpile for other deals. The suggested provisions are not necessarily the only ones nor the best ones. Again, the goal is to give the reader a general familiarity with the kinds of items which he or she will see in the market. Please be sure to study the section of this book called "Good Asks" to see some other ways and means to approach leasing issues in a RFP.

Tip:

Do the Math. Because leases are often long, the compounding effect can have significant economic impact. If you are not comfortable with the numbers, get a co-worker or friend to check your calculations. Knowing the dollar values can really help you prioritize your deal points.

RFP FORM

_____

_____

Date:

Re: _____

Dear _____:

As the exclusive real estate representative for _____ ("Tenant"), we have been authorized to present this Request for Proposal for the lease of the above Premises ("Premises") from _____ ("Landlord"):

Commencement Date:	The Commencement date will be the later of (a) _____ or (b) _____ days following Landlord's delivery of the Premises.
Initial Term:	_____ (____) years
Early Access Period:	Tenant will have early access to begin the installation of fixtures and fit up on or before the earlier of _____ or full lease execution. No Base Rent, operating expenses, or other amounts are payable by Tenant until _____.

Annual Base Rent/
Rent Abatement: Please (1) provide the Annual Base Rent for the Initial Term along with any projected rent increases, and (2) set out rent abatement available at the beginning of the lease.

Operating Expenses and
Real Estate Taxes: Tenant will pay operating expenses and property taxes. Provide an estimated itemization detailing operating expense components or CAM costs for which Tenant will be responsible for the first lease year.

Insurance: Please describe the types and cost of insurance required of Tenant.

Audit Rights: Tenant will have the right to inspect and audit the Landlord's books and records to confirm operating expenses. If discrepancies exceed 5%, Landlord will reimburse the Tenant for the costs of its audit.

Expense Increases Cap: Controllable expenses increases to be capped at ___% per year. Increases in taxes resulting from a sale of the Premises will not be borne by Tenant.

Tax Appeals: Tenant will have the right to contest Real Estate taxes throughout the term.

Inducements:	Please describe any inducements which Landlord will provide to Tenant.
Renewal Options:	Tenant requires ___ (_), ____ (_) year Renewal Options. Renewal Options shall be exercised not later than six (6) months before the expiration of the then-current Term. This right will not be personal to Tenant. The Annual Base Rent for Tenant's Renewal Option periods will be fixed for the first renewal option at _____ percent (_____%) of the then fair market rental rate for space of comparable size, quality and location to the Premises taking into account the rental abatements, tenant improvement allowance and any other inducements then given to new lessees in comparable space to the Premises, and shall consider the reduced brokerage commissions and rent abatement/build-out time involved in the renewal compared to other comparable transactions ("Market Rental Rate"). Tenant will have the right to submit the determination of Market Rental Rate to binding arbitration.
Utilities:	All utilities will be separately metered and installed by Landlord at Landlord's expense.
Security Deposit:	None
Tenant Buildout Requirements:	Tenant requires a turnkey proposal for improvements to be designed and constructed in accordance with mutually approved plans and drawings. Landlord will obtain all necessary permits, design and engineering services necessary to complete the Tenant's requirements as part of its proposal.

Parking: Provide a description of all available parking.

Facility Maintenance: Tenant will be responsible for ordinary interior maintenance, including routine system maintenance, trash removal, and janitorial services.

Landlord will be responsible for the repairs, maintenance and replacement of all structural building elements, including, without limitations, sprinkler system, the roof and roof membrane, exterior walls, foundations, floors, exterior landscaping etc. These items are not to be included in the CAM charge.

Landlord will also be responsible at its cost (excluded from CAM charge) for any repair and replacements of HVAC and other mechanical, plumbing and electrical, lighting, and parking lot. Landlord will warrant that all of the above items will be in good working condition on the Lease Commencement Date.

Assignment & Sublease: Subject to Landlord's consent, not to be unreasonably withheld or delayed, Tenant may sublease or assign any portion of the Premises. Tenant will retain all profits from such transactions(s).

Holdover:	Tenant may holdover for up to six (6) consecutive one-month periods following Lease expiration, on the same terms and conditions as provided in the Lease. After that period, rates shall not exceed 125% of existing rates.
Signage:	Tenant shall be entitled to the following signage rights: _____
Owner:	Please identify the legal owner of the premises and the ownership structure. Also advise as to the financing and financial strength of Landlord and provide contact information for Landlord.
Environmental:	Landlord will warrant and represent that the Premises and building are free of mold, asbestos and other hazardous and/or toxic materials. Landlord will provide Tenant with all copies of existing environmental reports. Landlord, at its sole cost and expense, will be responsible for any environmental issues not brought on to the site or premises by Tenant throughout the term of the lease and any subsequent renewal terms.
ADA:	Landlord will warrant the building and the Premises are in compliance with the requirements of the American with Disabilities Act and any other codes and/or laws. Landlord will be responsible for all future work and costs to comply with any future changes.
Landlord's Lien:	No Landlord's lien on any Tenant assets.

Tenant Alterations: Tenant may make interior alterations and changes in the Premises without Landlord's consent. Tenant will obtain Landlord's prior written approval for alterations affecting the mechanical systems, floor, roof or other structural components of the Premises. Tenant may, at its option, remove any leasehold improvements and will have the right to remove its fixtures at the expiration of the Lease.

Restoration: Tenant will have no obligation to restore the Premises or to remove any Landlord approved alterations at the end of the term. Tenant will leave the Premises in broom clean condition, normal wear and tear excepted.

Confidentiality: Landlord will not issue any public announcement, press release or other public disclosure regarding this Request for Proposal or its subject matter, the parties or the Lease without Tenant's prior written consent.

Non-Disturbance: Landlord will provide Tenant with Non-Disturbance Agreements in a form acceptable to Tenant from any ground lessors, mortgage holders or lien holders, of Landlord.

No Relocation Rights: Landlord will not have the right to relocate the Tenant.

Broker Representation: Upon the execution and delivery of the Lease by the parties, Landlord shall pay commission per a separate commission agreement between Landlord and _____.

Non-Binding: This Proposal is an invitation to commence negotiations with Tenant. It is not a legally binding document and creates no duty of good faith negotiation. Any agreement between Landlord and Tenant is subject to approval and execution of a formal lease document by Landlord and Tenant. Tenant may be simultaneously presenting requests for proposals to others. Tenant reserves the right at any time to accept any proposal or to submit any proposal without further notice to you or any other potential Landlord. Further, Tenant can withdraw from negotiations at any time for any or no reason.

Please provide your response to this RFP on or before _____, 20_____.

Sincerely,

_____

AREA ANALYSIS SCORING

A Tenant Representative Broker may need to educate a prospect (especially one coming from out of town) on local communities to help focus the search for potential sites. Many brokers have very sophisticated systems or software to assist with this process. This form represents a fairly simple approach.

The categories shown here are only a sample of possible criteria. They are not necessarily targeted to the type of use much less the individual tenant, but are mainly included to give some idea of which items will be important. This particular template compares three separate submarkets, each with certain advantages and drawbacks. The scoring is not weighted. All categories are treated equally.

Note that some may prefer a weighted approach with, for example, some categories counting for 5% of the total, others for twice that, etc.

	AREA A	AREA B	AREA C
NAME			
ZIP CODE			
EASE OF VEHICULAR ACCESS			
POPULATION WITHIN 5 MILE RADIUS			
RATE OF CHANGE IN POPULATION			
AVERAGE COMMUTE TIME			
LOCAL AMENITIES			
LOCAL TAXATION			
HOUSEHOLDS WITH INCOME FROM $80K-$120K (5 MILE RADIUS)			
HOUSEHOLDS WITH INCOME UNDER $80K (5 MILE RADIUS)			
MEDIAN HOUSEHOLD INCOME			
PROXIMITY TO MASS TRANSIT			
PROXIMITY TO CUSTOMERS			
PRESTIGE			
LOCAL GOVERNMENT INCENTIVES			
WALKABILITY			
OTHER			
TOTAL			
*SCORE FROM 1-10; 10 IS THE HIGHEST			

SMART ASKS

The following sets out a series of suggested additions to an RFP. Because the parties are not at the formal drafting stage, these are written in general terms. The aim is to pin down essential points as well as to obtain similar offers for different sites on a uniform basis to aid decision-making. Many suggestions are based on the rule that it (usually) never hurts to ask. Naturally, there are exceptions, and you must use good sense and tact, but you can assist your client sometimes by adding a creative "ask" to the mix. Some of these ideas have significant impact. They are not necessarily unfair to the landlord, but can yield economic or quality of tenancy benefits for the client.

The downside of using an RFP derives primarily from the way in which landlords react to them. Some landlords find this to be time consuming and obnoxious. Others, however, may require them. They are not offers, but may be invitations to get into a competition and they can be seen as obstacles to a negotiation. Thus, the Broker might try to educate the client and advocate for the RFP itself to be as inviting as possible. For example, where the prospective tenant has strong credit, furnishing information to that effect can help break down barriers.

The following cross a wide range of deals and situations. Clearly they don't all fit any one deal. These ideas have been collected from many savvy lessees, attorneys and Brokers.

AMENITIES AND SPECIAL RIGHTS

- **Building Amenities**

    Idea: As part of the "apples to apples" approach try to obtain the maximum information on special distinctive amenities.

    Example in RFP: "Please detail any distinctive or unique Building amenities such as Wi-Fi, special security, social club, rooftop deck, boardroom, car charging stations, bicycle racks, auditorium, conference facilities, cafeteria, private or executive dining, food catering, tenant lounge, health club, emergency power etc. that can be made available for Tenant's use. Describe the cost (if any) for such amenities."

- **Signage**

    Idea: Bend the signage issue in Tenant's favor at the earlier stage so Landlord will deal with it proactively and your client will not be forced into a Lease without adequate signage. In some deals this is an important issue and comparison of signage rights at competing sites can determine which leases get signed.

    Example in RFP: "Tenant will be granted exclusive Building exterior signs in compliance with Tenant's standard requirements. Tenant will determine the location, size, style and color subject to Landlord's reasonable approval and local building and architectural control standards. In addition to the primary signage on the Building, Tenant, at Landlord's expense, shall be provided identity in the Building which shall include appropriate signage at elevator lobbies and on entrance doors to all space(s) leased by Tenant."

    Issues to consider: Landlord may be unwilling to commit to excessive signage and may want to cut back to "best efforts" and limit the amount and types of signs.

- **Roof Rights and Communications**

    Idea: Obtain the maximum rights and specific locations for satellite dishes and other communications etc.

    Example in RFP: "Tenant at its expense, but at no added rent, shall have the right at any time during the Lease term to locate, install and maintain satellite dishes, telecommunication antennas, microwave and other equipment on the roof or in the Building. Tenant shall also have a free access to service/maintain this equipment 24 hours per day, 365 days per year. To access the roof, Tenant shall have the right to run cabling through the building's core and raceways. Tenant will be allowed to bring fiber optic services into the Building and the Premises. Installation will be subject to the approval of Landlord, not to be unreasonably withheld, conditioned or delayed."

    Issues to consider: Landlord will likely want to protect against any damages to the roof and may ask to limit locations and protect its warranty.

- **Parking**

    Idea: There are many potential issues which Tenant's needs to tackle on parking. This particular clause addresses some prime ones.

    Example in RFP: "The Property will have at least _____ spaces per 1000 square feet of leasable space. This ratio will be maintained throughout the term of the Lease; Tenant may terminate if the ratio is not satisfied. Further, Landlord will not interfere with traffic patterns in the parking area and will not change the striping of parking areas within ____ feet of Tenant's premises. In addition there never will be a charge for parking. Further, Tenant will receive ___ reserved spaces in a mutually agreed- upon area which is close to Tenant's premises."

Issues to consider: Landlord will be concerned if the parking ratios currently exceed the legal requirement and will believe it unfair for Tenant to insist on a more liberal standard. Landlord may want to limit its obligations to legal compliance. Also Landlord will not want to cede its control over parking arrangements.

- **Co-Tenancy**

    Idea: This is a creature of retail. The concept usually involves an anchor tenant. The Tenant will argue that it can only make money if Landlord retains the anchor [think, Kroger, Wal-Mart, etc.]. If the anchor goes away, Tenant may wish to leave as well.

    Example in RFP: "The following are Key Tenants: [LIST]. If at any time any of the Key Tenants are not open for business and operating at the Property then Tenant may, at its option either pay Alternative Rent or terminate the Lease. Alternative Rent is _____% of the annual Base Rent in the Lease."

    Issues to consider: The above is a particularly tough variation since it contains a death penalty (termination right) and no cure period. Landlord will, at the very least, seek to ameliorate.

- **LEED Certification**

    Idea: Sometimes LEED Certification will be meaningful.

    Example in RFP: "Is the Building LEED-certified? Detail this. If not fully certified please describe any LEED-certified features."

ASSIGNMENT AND BORROWING

- **Get Sublease Right**

    Idea: Landlord may be more amenable to future subleasing concessions at the RFP stage – before lawyers get involved. And by pre-negotiating the "profits" and offering a fair split Tenant can avoid battling a Landlord "standard provision."

    Example in RFP: "Tenant shall have the right to sublease all or a portion of the Premises. Landlord and Tenant shall any profits gained from the sublease on a 50/50 basis."

    Issues to consider: Landlord will resist the idea of Tenant competing with it and making a profit in Landlord's own business, i.e. leasing space. At the minimum, most Landlords will want to prevent any subletting to other lessees of the building or any prospective business with which Landlord is dealing.

- **Non-Disturbance**

    Idea: Stake your position as to non-disturbance at the early stages of negotiation. Make sure Landlord starts working on this immediately.

    Example in RFP: "Landlord shall obtain from the holder of any existing or future mortgage or deed of trust a commercially reasonable subordination, non-disturbance and attornment agreement in a form acceptable to Tenant which provides that in the event of foreclosure or a transfer in lieu thereof, Tenant will not be disturbed in its possession of the Premises and the Lease shall continue in full force and effect upon all its terms, covenants, conditions and obligations so long as no default has occurred by Tenant under the Lease

    which has not been cured within applicable cure periods and Tenant attorns to the purchaser or transferee as Landlord under the Lease. If Landlord does not provide the non-disturbance and attornment agreements(s), Tenant will not be required to subordinate or attorn to the Mortgagee(s) and the Lease shall be superior to/its/their interest(s)."

Issues to consider: Landlord will not want to go too far down the road with lender unless it knows Tenant is a serious prospect.

- **Assignment**

    Idea: Reduce the issues presented by the assignment clause as much as possible.

    Example in RFP: "Landlord's consent to assignment/sublease will not be unreasonably withheld, conditioned or delayed. Tenant will be released from further liability on any assignment and no consent will be needed for assignment/sublease to affiliates, related parties and successors or purchasers of Tenant or its business/assets. Business and stock/membership/partner assignment and transfer are not assignments for consent purposes. Any excess proceeds from assignment or sublease to be retained by Tenant."

    Issues to consider: Landlord will be concerned with downgrade in its Tenant quality. It will also be especially difficult to obtain the automatic release from liability. The back and forth on that can sometimes be broken by a provision that the release is available only if the assignee has a net worth in excess of a stipulated standard. Landlords also don't like Tenant retaining assignment/sublease "profits" and will resist or suggest a 50/50 split.

- **Assignment etc.**

    Idea: This is another version to obtain concessions in assignment language.

Example in RFP: "Tenant shall have the right at any time to assign or sublease or otherwise permit occupancy (collectively "transfer") of all or any portion of the Premises to any entity which is controlled by Tenant or which controls or is under common control of Tenant or any of its related parties. Also, Tenant may transfer the Lease to any successor entity, whether by merger, consolidation or otherwise, and to any entity that purchases all or substantially all of the Tenant's assets. No such sublease, assignment or other transaction requires Landlord's approval or consent and Tenant shall have the right to keep all of the profit, if any, therefrom.

Tenant also will have the right at any time to assign or sublease all or any portion of the Premises to any unrelated entities, subject to Landlord's prior written consent, which shall not be unreasonably withheld, conditioned or delayed. In the event of a sublease or assignment, any net profits shall belong to the benefit of Tenant. Landlord will also grant, (and cause each of its lenders to grant), to any assignee and each subtenant of Tenant, a recognition and non-disturbance agreement. Landlord has no right to recapture in the case of any assignment or sublease."

Issues to consider: Landlord may be averse to the blanket changes included in this language.

- **Tenant Lender Issues**

    Idea: Tenants often will need the Landlord to assist in connection with specific lender requirements. Two areas of particular concern are (1) the need by lender to get the consent of Landlord confirming that lender has a first and only lien on collateral backing its loan – furniture, fixtures etc. and (2) lender wishes for the right to take over the Lease.

    Example in RFP: "Landlord agrees to consent to Tenant's grant of a leasehold mortgage right to its lender(s). Landlord will execute necessary documents as required by such lender(s). Such consents will be provided on a timely expedited basis and may include provisions giving lender(s) the right to (a) retain first liens on inventory, equipment, furniture, fixture and other collateral (b) retain possession of the premises for at least ninety (90) days after the Lease ends to permit lender to remove/sell/deal with collateral (c) receive reasonable notice of default from Landlord (d) cure default under the Lease and (e) enter into a new Lease with Landlord."

Issues to consider: Some Landlords will be wary of such broad rights and such general terms and will at the least want this to be subject to Landlord's satisfaction with such provisions in its sole discretion. Also, Landlord will not want to grant the lender a right to hold over in space for long and will want rent/utilities reimbursement for such period of time.

CONSTRUCTION AND MAINTENANCE

- **Control Construction**

    Idea: Tenant may wish to have a higher level of control over the construction of space, particularly in complex or expensive situations. Also, Tenant wants to limit supervisory charges of Landlord.

    Example in RFP: "Tenant may retain its own project manager and general contractor for the construction and project management of the buildout as well as any future alterations/improvements. Landlord will not be paid a fee for supervision or management of the construction either initially or later in the term."

- **Allowances**

    Idea: Ask for as many allowances as your client desires. Remember allowances have tax consequences so let Tenant have final say in determining whether to seek allowances, free rent etc. If the allowance is to be paid back (in rent) make the language clear.

Example in RFP: "Landlord will provide a Tenant Improvement Allowance of $_____. Such Tenant Improvement Allowance may be utilized for construction of improvements and all other occupancy-related expenses including, without limitation, moving expenses, space design, project management fees, signage, telecommunication and cabling, architectural services, security systems and furniture along with other expenses deemed appropriate by Tenant. The Tenant Improvement Allowance will be disbursed following Tenant's submission of a requisition and any supporting documentation reasonably required by Landlord. Landlord shall pay the amount of the requisition (up to the amount of the Tenant Improvement Allowance) within ten (10) days of receipt. Any unused portion of this Allowance may be used by Tenant to offset rent."

- **Duty to Give Possession**

    Idea: The Landlord's form Lease normally will have language which is open ended in terms of providing Tenant possession at the Lease inception. On its face the Landlord often is not subject to penalty for late turnover of the space. Tenant needs to plan for move in and cannot be left in an open-ended twilight zone.

    Example in RFP: "If the Premises are delivered after _____, Tenant will be entitled to free rent (Base and Additional) on a day for day basis for the first _____ days of delivery. After such ____ day period Tenant shall have the option to either (a) receive a rent credit of $_____ for each day of delay thereafter or (b) terminate this Lease."

    Issues to consider: Landlord will want to push back on several issues. First, it will want to carve out delays caused by Tenant and force majeure delays. Second, it will want to extend the period before rent is credited and probably wish to call for Tenant to give written notice of some period before the penalty kicks in. Finally, Landlord will seek to strike any termination right as too punitive.

- **Tenant Improvement Budget**

    Idea: This clause is a detailed buildout clause which among other things calls for Landlord to give a budget in advance. This language is fit for a "big deal" where the improvements are pretty well industry-known and easy to deal with in terms of pricing. The clause also drops in some allowance concessions and seeks to saddle Landlord with most duties from the RFP onward.

    Example in RFP: "Please describe Landlord's proposed budget for the required Tenant Improvements (TI's) and confirm that Landlord will accept the risk of cost overruns if the proposed budget is insufficient to complete the improvements."

    Regarding change orders, if during the construction process Tenant requires additional TI's, then Landlord agrees to provide the additional funds to the TI budget. Landlord will provide a budget to Tenant for approval in writing for such change orders before the commencement of TI's construction. Please specify the formula that will be used to determine the rent rate charges as a result of the additional TI's.

    Tenant requires a discretionary allowance of $_____ to be used for moving and fit-up requirements at Tenant's sole discretion. If Tenant does not utilize the allowance or any portion thereof, specify the formula that will be used to determine the reduction to the year one lease rate or specify that Tenant may use such amount for any other items it selects.

    Landlord shall secure and pay for all architectural/space planning, permits, governmental fees (including fire department/sprinkler inspection fees), licenses and inspections necessary for the proper execution, completion and approval of the Tenant Improvements. Landlord shall certify that the Tenant Improvements are in compliance with all laws, ordinances, rules, regulations, codes and orders of any city, state, or federal authority bearing on the performance and approval of the work. Further, Landlord shall assume full responsibility, shall bear all costs and expenses, and indemnify and hold Tenant harmless with regard to the completion of any improvements, which violate laws, ordinances, codes, rules and regulations. Tenant may, but is not required to have a representative on site to review construction progress."

- **Hoisting Charges (Industrial)**

    Idea: Some facilities have limited availability of freight elevators. They do not wish to dedicate them primarily to a particular user. Some may seek to impose a hoisting charge to cover costs. The clause gains the upper hand for a Tenant seeking to move-in a large installation.

    Example in RFP: "Please confirm that Landlord and/or its contractors will not impose any charges for utilizing the Building's freight elevator(s) or outside hoist during the construction of Tenant's space both during the initial move into the space and for at least _____ days after move-in."

- **HVAC Work**

    Idea: Make the Landlord pay for substantial HVAC Work which will tend to benefit the building in the long run and may outlive the tenancy.

    Example in RFP: "Tenant will only be responsible for ordinary repairs and maintenance of HVAC. Any expenditure in connection with HVAC over $500 will be borne by Landlord."

    Issues to consider: Landlord may counter by suggesting that Tenant should at least pay for the proportionate share of costs of repair and replacement pro-rated based on the useful life of the equipment relating to the remaining term of the Lease.

- **HVAC Overtime**

    Idea: HVAC charges for after-hours can turn into a significant costs for Tenant. At the RFP stage Tenant may wish to introduce some protective concepts.

    Example in RFP: "Any overtime HVAC charges will (a) be allocated among all simultaneous users and (b) be discounted by ____% should Tenant use more than ____ hours in any month. Tenant will also be treated as a "most favored nation" and will never be charged more for HVAC then the lowest rate charged to any other lessee of the Property."

    Issue to consider: Landlord will not want to allocate these costs and may tend to prefer to settle on a lower number/hour.

- **Space Planning Allowance**

    Idea: One possible concession involves an additional allowance for space planning.

    Example in RFP: "Landlord shall provide, in addition to the Tenant Improvement Allowance, a reasonable allowance for initial space planning and up to two (2) revisions, to be performed by an architect of Tenant's choice, regardless of whether a Lease is ultimately executed by Tenant. Landlord will provide a written commitment confirming its willingness to bear this cost."

    Issues to consider: Note that this calls for Landlord to spend money on planning even if there is not a Lease. Some Landlords will want to cap the amount and some will want reimbursement if the deal doesn't get completed. Some, naturally, will just say no.

GENERAL AND OPERATIONS

- **Reasonableness Standard**

    Idea: Get a general clause which will require Landlord to be reasonable in granting consents, charging fees and the like.

    Example in RFP: "Consents and approvals under the Lease will not be unreasonably withheld, delayed or conditioned. Failure to respond within ten (10) days of request is deemed approval. All fees and expenses shall be limited to those which are reasonable, actual and out of pocket."

    Issues to consider: Landlord's concern is that the reasonableness standard is an invitation to litigation and takes away its sovereignty over its property.

- **Full Time Access and Security**

    Idea: Get the Landlord to provide that access is always available to the space – not just when the Building is open. Also confirm that security will be on site 24/7.

    Example in RFP: "Tenant shall have access twenty-four (24) hours per day, seven (7) days per week, fifty-two (52) weeks per year to the Premises and parking facilities. Security will be provided at the Premises and parking facilities during those same time periods."

- **Use**

    Idea: It is a good idea to expand the use clause to be as broad as possible.

    Example in RFP: "Permitted use is [_____] along with any lawful use."

Issues to consider: Landlord may push back on a generic language use clause. Tenant will want to seek to avoid restrictions – try to get "office" rather than "medical office." For example, seek a right to preserve the right for incidental ancillary uses.

- **Exclusive Use**

    Idea: Retail Tenants will want to be insulated from competition as much as possible.

    Example in RFP: "Tenant will be granted an exclusive use by Landlord which will include the Property in which the Premises is located and will extend to any location within a five (5) mile radius of the Premises. This covenant will bind Landlord and its affiliates from directly or indirectly permitting any space in such radius to be used or occupied for the sale of any of the following: [Describe]"

    Issues to consider: Landlord will seek to limit the clause so that Landlord's duty will be not to Lease for the exclusion area – i.e., it may resist clauses which make it the "policeman." And Landlord will not like extending to other related entities and other locations.

- **Continuation of Services**

    Idea: Landlord form leases nearly always exempt Landlord from liability – even if the essential building services are down indefinitely. A Tenant may wish to obtain less onerous language.

    Example in RFP: "If essential building services are disrupted or unavailable for more than three (3) consecutive days the rent will be abated until full restoration is carried out. If such essential building services are disrupted or unavailable for more than fifteen (15) days in any sixty (60) day period Tenant will have the right to notify Landlord of its intent to terminate the Lease and if Landlord fails to correct the issue within fifteen (15) days thereafter Tenant will have the right to terminate."

Issued consider: Landlord will likely stonewall, but may accept middle ground involving more time to cure, limited abatement and no right to terminate.

- **Self-Insurance**

    Idea: Large Tenants will be interested in preserving the right to self-insure.

    Example in RFP: "Notwithstanding anything to the contrary contained in the Lease, the Tenant may satisfy its insurance obligations by self-insurance, provided Tenant has a net worth in excess of $150,000,000. Any self-insurance maintained by Tenant shall be deemed to contain all of the terms and conditions applicable to such insurance, including, without limitation, a deemed waiver of subrogation. If Tenant elects to self-insure then with respect to any claims which may result from incidents occurring during the Lease Term, such self-insurance obligation shall survive the expiration or earlier termination of this Lease to the same extent as the customarily required insurance would survive."

- **No Operating Covenant**

    Idea: To make clear that Tenant can stop its operations without any default. It also aims to prevent land use restrictions.

    Example in RFP: "There shall be no operating covenants. Tenant shall not be in default for vacating the Premises so long as Tenant pays its rent per the Lease and is not in default of other provisions. Further, there shall be no special deed restrictions or land use restrictions."

MISCELLANEOUS

- **Brokerage**

    Idea: There is no reason to start off with a misunderstanding by Landlord and/or its Broker as to payment of commission.

    Example in RFP: "This RFP is submitted based on the understanding that _____ will receive 6% total gross rent as commission from Landlord, paid on Lease execution and in accordance with the terms and conditions set forth on the attached Commission Agreement."

- **Confidentiality**

    Idea: Tenant will benefit from an ability to limit Landlord disclosure during the negotiation. Besides keeping the Landlord from stirring up its existing tenants to take the space it allows your client to protect its employee and Landlord relationships.

    Example in RFP: "Landlord and its agents agree to keep this RFP's existence and subsequent negotiations between the Landlord and Tenant involving a possible Lease of the Premises (the "Negotiations") in confidence and shall not at any time disclose or permit the disclosure of the existence or substance of these negotiations to any person, without, first obtaining the prior written consent of Tenant. Notwithstanding the foregoing, Landlord may disclose the existence of the Negotiations to (i) its legal counsel, accountants, lenders and engineers who need to be aware of the existence of the negotiation and (ii) Landlord may disclose the negotiations to the extent that such disclosure is required by law or court order, but in such a situation, Landlord must first provide as much advance written notice to Tenant as possible."

Issues to consider: Landlords fear consequences of unintended disclosure. Further this clause is one-sided.

- **No Security Deposit**

    Idea: Just say no in advance.

    Example in RFP: "Tenant will not pay a Security Deposit."

- **Security Deposit**

    Idea: If Tenant cannot avoid a Security Deposit it may wish to work on burn-off in the RFP.

    Example in RFP: "Provided Tenant is not in default beyond all applicable cure periods the Security Deposit will be reduced by _____ on the _____ month following the Lease Commencement Date."

    Issues to consider: Landlord may be willing to accept the argument that good performance by Tenant for a substantial time is a justification for a reduction. On the other hand, Landlord will probably want to revoke the privilege immediately in the case of any late payment or other breach and may want to require the Security Deposit be reinstated at original levels should such breach occur.

- **Rules and Regulations**

    Idea: Rules and Regulations tend to be ignored by many Tenants and Brokers, but these can be impactful, particularly when there is language which allows them to be revised freely from time to time. Because these are also a part of the Lease, Landlord can effectively have free rein to change the deal.

    Example in RFP: "Landlord shall enforce its rules and regulations in a non-discriminatory manner; if Tenant requests Landlord will enforce them against other lessees.

Any new rule or regulation must (a) be reasonable (b) require Tenant's approval and (c) never adversely affect Tenant's use and enjoyment of its Premises or increase its costs of operations."

- **No Relocation**

    Idea: Avoid the negotiation. Reject relocation out of hand.

    Example in RFP: "Landlord may not relocate Tenant during the term of the Lease or any extension."

- **Tenant Remedies**

    Idea: Many Leases are silent vis-à-vis Tenant remedies.

    Example in RFP: "The Lease will include meaningful rights and remedies for Tenant in the case of Landlord default or breach a Landlord's representations or warranties. These will include (a) set off; (b) the right to cure Landlord's defaults after notice with setoff of all costs including interest and a reasonable administrative fee; (c) termination in the event of material default or representation/warranty failure; and (d) rent abatement for defaults affecting use and enjoyment."

    Issues to consider: Landlords will push back on set-off and termination. An argument you can offer in this early part of the Lease courtship: "Treat my Tenant right and this will never come up anyway."

- **Tenant's Form**

    Idea: Get the Landlord to give up control of the Lease document by an early introduction to "our standard form" or at least "our standard addendum."

Example in RFP: "Tenant requires that its Lease form [or standard addendum] be used as the documentation of the Lease."

Issues to consider: Landlords prefer to use their own form for multiple reasons, not the least of which is familiarity, reducing legal fees and lender form requirements. That said, a Tenant with some economic muscle may seek to control the playing field. Landlords sometimes will tell their lawyer to "just get the deal done" if the tenant is needed/wanted badly enough.

- **Background Information**

    Idea: Get a head start on due diligence and, if the RFP aims to compare properties be able to size up the age/quality/future of various properties.

    Example in RFP: "Landlord should provide a full description of its background and experience and that of its manager. Also, please confirm the year of construction of the Building and parking lot and additions including details on Landlord's plans for refurbishing or improving them. In addition, to assist the Tenant in its evaluation, please provide all information you have regarding environmental matters at the property and regarding its condition, including, without limitation, structural, mechanical and soils conditions, the presence and location of asbestos, PCB transformers and any other toxic, hazardous or contaminated substances and underground storage tanks, in, on, or about the property. Supplement with information on other tenants and the demographics of the property."

- **Utility Information**

    Idea: Some choices of space will be driven by utility costs and availability. Here is a typical information request in an RFP. More detailed or specific clauses can be tailored to meet individual Tenant situations.

Example in RFP: "Please indicate the providers of electric and gas (include both the commodity supplier as well as the distributor) and telephone utility services for the Building. Provide any information regarding substations or power grids that serve the Property. Provide a complete description on the building's emergency power system. In addition describe any generator or existing equipment currently available to Tenant and add any further information which may help Tenant differentiate between this Building and others."

- **Financing Contingency**

    Idea: Some Tenants will need to get the Lease finished before they can complete financing.

    Example in RFP: "Tenant's Lease obligations will be contingent upon Tenant receiving financing for the business from a reputable lender on terms acceptable to the Tenant in Tenant's sole and absolute discretion."

    Issues to consider: This will be very difficult for Landlord. Landlord will feel that it is being held hostage – committed to a deal with only Tenant having an out. Landlord will, in the face of this clause, likely insist on a more data on Tenant's current loan prospects and will need an outside time limit. Landlord may suggest it will have the right to terminate the Lease any time before Tenant releases the contingency.

- **Right to Offset**

    Idea: Put right of offset into the RFP. If it is a competitive bid process certain Landlords will accede to this language.

    Example in RFP: "If Landlord fails to perform any of its obligations under the Lease, Tenant, after written notice to Landlord and a fifteen (15) business day cure period, will have the right to perform such obligations and then offset the related costs against rental payments due under the Lease. This right will not apply if the cure would reasonably take longer than fifteen (15) business days to cure and Landlord has commenced to cure and is diligently pursuing the cure toward timely completion. Tenant will use good faith efforts to pursue reasonable measures to cure at a reasonable cost.

Issues to consider: Landlord will typically oppose any offset right. And it may be restricted from doing so by its mortgage.

- **Proposal Only**

    Idea: While a RFP is clearly just that, given the litigious nature of our world, it may help to add a special disclaimer.

    Example in RFP: "This Request for Proposal is for informational purposes only, and is not intended to be binding on the parties. It is merely an effort to obtain information and evaluate sites. It shall not be construed as an offer or option to lease. Any obligations of Tenant to proceed with a lease transaction is dependent on the execution and delivery of the appropriate lease agreement by Landlord and Tenant. This in no way constitutes an agreement to negotiate and Tenant may terminate discussions or negotiations at any time without any liability or obligation whatsoever."

OPERATING EXPENSES AND TAXES

- **Background re: Operating Expense**

    Idea: Here's a typical effort to gather information on operating expenses and establish ground rules. Note (c) would help to know if a gross-up is used:

    Example in RFP: "Tenant will be responsible for its pro-rata share of Real Property Taxes and Operating Expenses. Please provide the following:

a. A breakdown of the operating expense and tax figures that have been budgeted for the first year and the following lease year noting the estimated occupancy level and real estate tax assessment percentage for each year.

b. The estimated and actual operating expenses for the past three (3) years.

c. Indicate whether the current real estate tax expense reflects a fully occupied building. Is "gross-up" used?

d. A 3% annual cap on future increase of controllable operating expense will be required.

e. Show calculation for deriving the pro-rata share of operating and tax expenses.

f. Tenant will have the right to audit the Landlord's books and records as to tax as an operating expense."

- **Operating Expense Exclusion**

    Idea: Operating Expenses can be a significant area for economic give and take. The following approval aims at getting the Landlord to surrender to the Tenant's standard language at the RFP stage.

    Example in RFP: "The attached list of Exclusions from Operating Expenses will be part of the Lease"

    Issues to consider: Landlords tend to dislike the imposition of Tenant language both from an economic standpoint and from an administrative point of view. For example management must calculate each "custom" Lease costs separately. This lends to significant effort, time and possibility for error.

- **Moving/Fixturing etc. Allowance**

    Idea: A highly desired Tenant can sometimes get a bucket of concessions making these "gives" look like expectations.

    Example in RFP: "Tenant requires that Landlord provide an Allowance of $____ per foot to assist Tenant with its moving costs, FF&E and telecommunications/cabling costs."

- **Cap on Operating Expenses**

    Idea: The Tenant's ability to budget and plan is enhanced if the majority of operating costs are limited in as many ways as possible. There are a huge number of variations on the procedure. One is to try and hit hard with a very tight RFP clause.

    Example in RFP: "Tenant's payment obligation for all Operating Expenses, excluding taxes, utilities and insurance, shall never increase by more than three (3%) per annum."

    Issues to consider: Landlord will likely push back. The carve out for non-controllables does not include snow and ice removal for example. Also, 3% is very low and the clause is not cumulative – thus, if costs stay stable and there is a big spike in one year Landlord will bear most of the pain "forever."

- **Audit of Operating Expenses**

    Idea: Tenant will want meaningful review of expenses – often broader than the narrow provisions typical of Landlord form Leases.

    Example in RFP: "Operating Expense audit rights will be granted to Tenant and the Lease will give Tenant reasonable time to exercise such rights. Tenant will be permitted to review and copy all documents at no additional expense and audit rights will extend at least three (3) years.

Errors in operating expenses over 3% or errors in property taxes in excess of 1% will trigger reimbursement by Landlord of the audit cost. Audit rights will survive Lease termination and if Tenant discover errors in any year it will the right to re-evaluate previous years."

- **Limit Management Fee**

    Idea: Sometimes Operating Expense negotiation are basically nonstarters – especially with intuitional Landlords. Sometimes a Tenant can at least get a few minor protective concession.

    Example in RFP: "In no event will the management fee for the Building (including line item administrative and management costs) exceed 3% of the net rental."

- **Real Estate Taxes**

    Idea: A large part of Operating Expenses is often dedicated to real estate taxes. There are several issues that require special attention. This clause deals with some of those issues and includes a somewhat controversial provision in connection with the effect of a sale on tax liability and construction.

    Example in RFP: "Real Estate Taxes will exclude penalties on interest, income tax or tax on Landlord's gross rent, gift and other taxes normally excluded and will not include increases resulting from construction during the Lease term which does not benefit leasees generally or which does not create additional proportionate rentable area. Increases resulting from any sale of property are excluded. Tenant will have the right to contest taxes and Landlord will cooperate to assure that any refunds are credited or paid to Tenant even after the end of the Lease."

    Issues to consider: Landlords are concerned about using language which prevents every tax dollar paid from being reimbursed. The exclusion for sale related increase will be very impactful on Landlord and will likely be rejected. Remember the Landlord will fear that the sale price could take a hit if a buyer loses the full "pass-through" of tax cost.

OPTIONS AND RIGHTS

- **Early Termination**

    Idea: Tenant has the right to end the Lease before its natural termination date if certain events occur or the space fails to work.

    Example in RFP: "At any time after year ____ of the Lease Tenant may exercise an early termination right by giving notice to Landlord at least sixty (60) days in advance of the date of early termination specified in the notice."

    Issues to consider: Landlord will at the least want to be reimbursed for unamortized TI, leasing commissions, etc.

- **Option for Additional Space**

    Idea: There are various mechanisms to foster future expansion. These can establish a security blanket for the expanding client. An Option for Additional Space can allow Tenant to budget and plan for an expansion in a better defined way than it can under a right of first refusal or right to first offer.

    Example in RFP: "Tenant shall have an ongoing option to expand into any available space in the building at the same terms and conditions of those existing in the Lease, with the same Tenant Improvements standard for the Initial Premises."

    Issues to consider: Landlord will not want to have this option hanging over its head and will either resist or seek to dramatically limit it. Any win here can yield real benefits for Tenant.

- **Right of First Refusal**

    Idea: Ideally Tenant will get a first refusal right on space which is to be let in the building (or at least adjacent space).

This can work well with a first option to keep control over future space needs.

Example in RFP: "Should Landlord wish to accept a third party Lease [_____] it will provide Tenant the option to lease such space on the business terms negotiated with such third party except that the Lease term for such space shall be contemporaneous with the Lease with Tenant. Tenant will have ten (10) business days to elect to accept such option. Should Tenant decline and Landlord does not complete such transaction, Tenant will be re-offered the space on the original terms. [If appropriate – "Nothing herein will adversely affect any option granted Tenant to lease such space and Tenant may elect to exercise its option to Lease under as described in this RFP instead of accepting a first refusal offer."]

Issues to consider: Landlord will feel its rights are limited. Expect resistance.

- **Extension Options**

    Idea: Not only get early commitment of Landlord to option, but also tilt the definition of "Fair Market Rent" in a way that favors the Tenant.

    Example in RFP: "Tenant shall have the right to extend the Lease for up to _____ (__) _____ (__) year option terms. Tenant may exercise its option(s) to extend by written notice to Landlord at least _____ (__) prior to the end of the initial term or option term as applicable. Landlord will provide an advisory notice so that options to extend are not lost without a notice. If options to extend are exercised, the terms and conditions of the Lease shall remain, except the Base Rent payable during each option term (as applicable) will be ninety five percent (95%) of the then-prevailing Fair Market Rent. Fair Market Rent of leases with tenants of comparable stature and all market concessions, including but not limited to comparable space, comparable buildings, rent, free rent, tenant improvement allowances, commissions and other inducements. There will be no "floor" on the option term rents. The Fair Market Rent will be determined by a disinterested appraiser if the parties cannot agree and if Tenant is not satisfied with the determination it may revoke its exercise. Options to extend are not personal to Tenant; they can be exercised by any assignee of the Lease."

Issues to consider: Landlord will want to have more control over the definition of Fair Market Rent and may also not want to have to give an advisory notice. Landlord may also question other rights included herein, including no floor on option Rents and a right by Tenant to pull its election.

STANDARDS AND COMPLIANCE

- **Landlord Obligation/Fire/Safety/ADA**

    Idea: Cause Landlord to deliver the best possible product. Eliminate many issues as to the quality and compliance of the Building/Premises.

    Example in RFP: "Prior to Lease Commencement, Landlord shall deliver in good working order the Project common areas, as well as the structural, mechanical, electrical, plumbing, fire/life/safety, and any other systems of the Building including the entire exterior and interior structure. Consistent with the normal maintenance and repair of a Class "A" building, Landlord shall keep in good order, condition and repair all mechanical, electrical and plumbing systems, and all equipment serving the Premises throughout the term and any extensions. Landlord shall be responsible for causing the common areas of the Building to comply with fire/life/safety legal requirements. Landlord shall also be responsible for ADA. Further, Landlord shall be responsible for continued compliance with all fire/life/safety requirements and ADA as it relates to the common areas throughout the term of the Lease and any extension."

- **Present and Future Compliance**

    Idea: This clause, from a "build to suit" proposal is aimed at making Landlord deliver a compliant Building. Also, future general compliance duties are by Landlord. However, note that this form tries to carve up the cost so that Landlord is not unfairly disadvantaged.

    Example in RFP: "Landlord will warrant that upon Lease commencement, the Building and parking will be in compliance with all laws, codes and rules in force at that time. Thereafter, Landlord shall pay for any expense or capital improvement required to be made to the Building resulting from any governmental law or regulation that was not applicable at the time the Building was constructed (but which is not a direct result of Tenant's specific use of the building) provided that the cost(s) of said improvement(s) shall be amortized over such period of time and in such manner as required under generally accepted accounting principles and the annual amount of such amortization shall be included in the operating expenses to be reimbursed by Tenant. Any improvement required which is a direct result of Tenant's use of the Building shall be the sole responsibility of Tenant."

- **Hazardous Material**

    Idea: Get this issue put to bed early. If Landlord is unhelpful then you will want to pay extra attention to the environmental issues and do the right due diligence in any case.

    Example in FRP: "Landlord will represent and warrant that there are no hazardous substances located in, on or under the Building, the property or Premises and there has been no violation of any law governing hazardous substances thereon. If hazardous substances are discovered at some later date on or about the Building or Premises, which were not caused by Tenant, the Landlord will be responsible for all costs and expenses associated with regulatory requirements to eliminate such problems, including asbestos, underground tanks etc. Landlord will indemnify, defend and hold harmless Tenant from pre-existing issues as well as anything after the Lease which does not arise from Tenant's negligence."

Issues to consider: This language is very broad. Landlord likely will seek to cut it back and make any representation subject to existing reports and its "knowledge."

- <u>Representation and Warranties</u>

    Idea: The Tenant might wish to ask the Landlord to represent and warrant certain essential items – shifting the due diligence concerns back to Landlord.

    Example in RFP: "Landlord shall represent and warrant the following: (a) The Property is properly zoned and Tenant's use is permitted under applicable law; (b) Landlord has good title to the Property which includes the Premises and there are no covenants, conditions or encumbrances which will adversely affect Tenant's use and enjoyment of the Premises; (c) the Premises and Property are in compliance with all applicable laws including ADA and there are no outstanding code violations; (d) There are no impact fees, hook-up fees or other fees or charges required with respect to the Premises; (e) Landlord will not require any third party consent to enter into the Lease; and (f) utility capacities are sufficient for Tenant's intended use."

    Issues to consider: The Landlord will often be wary of giving many reps. Also it will argue some of this is up to Tenant. For example the Landlord will argue that it is not in a position to represent utilities are sufficient – that is up to Tenant and its engineers to determine.

- <u>Structure/Latent Defects</u>

    Idea: Make it clear that those items that could not be discovered will be borne by Landlord.

Example in RFP: "Landlord, at its sole cost and expense, shall be 100% responsible for the repair of any structural and latent defects in the Building during the term of the Lease, including any extension and/or option periods. These expenses shall not be part of Operating Expenses."

Issues to consider: Landlord will want to make this part of Operating Expenses, if possible.

- **Environmental**

    Idea: Get due diligence started if you wish. Also, obtain Landlord's commitment to be responsible for existing environmental conditions.

    Example in RFP: "Landlord will promptly provide all environmental reports in Landlord's possession for Tenant to review. Landlord shall indemnify, defend and hold Tenant harmless from and against any and all claims, losses, and costs related to or arising from known and unknown hazardous substances or materials currently or later located in or introduced to the Premises, Building or Property by any party other than Tenant. Landlord shall immediately remediate any such hazardous substances or materials at its sole cost and expense."

    Issues to consider: Environmental can be an extremely sensitive area and open-ended language like this may make Landlord apprehensive. Landlord will probably want nondisclosure agreements and tighter language than this.

- **Approval Contingency**

    Idea: Tenants do not want to be held to a Lease if they are unable to get the necessary approvals, but they often need a Lease in hand to obtain those approvals. The Lease thus will require a post-execution contingency.

    Example in RFP: "The Lease shall be expressly contingent upon satisfactory resolution of all zoning issues and receipt of a building permit for _____ issued from the local governmental agency. Landlord shall be responsible for any required hearings or approvals required by the local municipality."

Issues to consider: Landlord will be concerned that it will spend a great deal of money and get close to the finish line only to lose a deal. Meanwhile it is no longer able to Lease. Landlord will want a time limit on this as well as some final commitment in hand to keep the Tenant honest.

SURRENDER

- **Define Removal on Termination; Removal of Cabling, etc.**

    Idea: Tenant will typically be required to remove trade fixtures, but may also be required to remove cables or other installations at the time of Lease termination. This can be a meaningful cost. Since it is a "future" event it may be glossed over in the glow of a new prospective deal.

    Example in RFP: "Tenant shall not be required to carry out any additional steps beyond removal of its furniture, trade fixtures and inventory and equipment at the time of Lease termination."

- **Restoration Limits**

    Idea: Limit the need to restore at the end of the Lease.

    Example in RFP: "No restoration shall be required at the end of the Lease Term or any extension for any initial Tenant Improvements or any alterations to the Premises made at any time which have been approved by the Landlord."

    Issues to consider: Landlord will, at the very least, want to specify Tenant will leave the Premises in broom clean condition.

TIMING AND TERMS AND PREMISES

- **Early Occupancy**

    Idea: The opportunity to get in and fixture space before any obligation to pay rent gives Tenant a big advantage in meeting deadlines.

    Example in RFP: "Tenant shall be permitted to enter the Premises after full Lease execution at no cost for the purpose of carrying out its work including, without limitation, installing its furniture systems, computer systems, telecommunications and cabling, fixtures and special improvements."

    Issues to consider: Landlord will want to make sure Tenant does not interfere with Landlord's build-out and may wish to start the clock on Tenant for certain costs like utilities.

- **Right to Re-measure**

    Idea: The cumulative effect of paying for incorrect space can be significant. Landlord will sometimes want you to "stipulate" to a figure – but what if it is wrong?

    Example in RFP: "Tenant shall have the right to re-measure and independently verify the square footage within _____ days of commencement. Discrepancies will be corrected by written memorandum setting out the proper square footage, rent, pro-rata share etc. In addition, Landlord will provide CAD drawings of both Premises and the Building with its response to this RFP and at time of any future demising."

    Issues to consider: Landlord wants to be able to project income on the Lease. A small discrepancy because of a mismeasurement or carpenter's error, is always possible. Landlord, thus may ask for a threshold amount – perhaps insisting on a revision of the Lease only it is off by "more than 5%" and then giving Landlord the right to revise the demised area accordingly.

- **Sidewalks/Exterior**

    Idea: If your client is a retailer or even another type of user which conducts special events or has outside promotions etc. you may want the right to use outside and beyond the Premises.

    Example in RFP: "Tenant will have the reasonable right to use the sidewalk and/or exterior areas for special installations and events from time to time."

- **Confirm Start Date**

    Idea: Define the Lease Commencement Date to Tenant's advantage early in the negotiation process.

    Example in RFP: "The Lease Commencement Date shall be the later of (a) _____ or b) _____ days following Landlord's delivery of the Premises to Tenant with Landlord's Work completed and ready for construction of the Tenant Improvement work by Tenant."

- **Holdover**

    Idea: Especially in shorter leases, holdover can arise before the parties have fully resolved their future plans. Form clauses can be very harsh. This aims to lessen the Landlord's "standard" provision.

    Example in RFP: "With sixty (60) days advance written notice, Tenant shall have the right to holdover for a period up to three (3) months after the expiration of the initial term or any extension at the same Base Rent as was in effect during the last month of the previous term. After that, the holdover Base Rent will be 110% of the Base Rent in effect during the last month of the previous term. Tenant will not be responsible for any damages beyond holdover rent (including, but not limited to, consequential damages) in the event of a holdover in the Premises."

Issues to consider: Landlord will be uncomfortable with any provision that may tie up its space and keep it from doing other deals. Also, 110% of Base Net is rather small. Many Landlords will want at least 125% and likely more.

SECTION IV: ADDITIONAL FORMS

"A landlord is showing a couple around an apartment. The husband looks up and says, "Wait a minute. This apartment doesn't have a ceiling." The landlord answers, "That's okay. The people upstairs don't walk around that much."

~ Gilbert Gottfried

CERTIFICATE OF SUBSTANTIAL COMPLETION

Sometimes Brokers are not paid all or part of their commission on a lease until after the lease actually starts. As a result it is helpful to the Broker and the parties to be sure of the start date of the lease.

Here are two examples of documents which the landlord and tenant can exchange to confirm the commencement date and other items. Often attorneys for the parties will have a form for this. These are two pretty generic forms. Either can be a tool to establish the date, to avoid any dispute between the parties and to definitively establish the date for payment of the commission (if applicable). Style of the form depends on the parties and circumstances.

Certificate of Substantial Completion Form

Landlord: _____

Lease Dated: _____

Tenant: _____

Building: _____

Premises: _____

This Certificate applies to the Tenant Improvements Work carried out by Landlord for the above Lease. Landlord, hereby certifies that the Landlord's portion of Tenant Improvement Work has been substantially completed on _____, 20__.

As a result of the above, the following dates shall apply under the Lease:
Commencement Date: _____
Rent Commencement Date: _____
Termination Date: _____

The parties confirm the above by signing below. Each signer is fully authorized to execute this Certificate. Facsimile or electronic/digital signatures are fully binding for all purposes.

TENANT

By: _____

Dated: _____

LANDLORD
By: _____

Dated: _____

Commencement Date Notice/Memorandum

Date: _____

Premises: _____

Tenant: _____

Landlord: _____

This is a Commencement Date Notice/Memorandum ("Memo") in connection with the Lease for the above Premises, dated _____ ("Lease"). The capitalized terms in this Memo have the same meaning given them in the Lease.

1. The Commencement Date is _____.

2. The Termination Date is _____.

3. The initial Base Rent is _____. Base Rent is payable on the _____ day of every month during the term in equal monthly installments of $_____ commencing on _____. The Rent Schedule will be as follows:

    [COMPLETE AS NEEDED]

4. Since the Commencement Date occurs on a day other than the first day of the calendar month, the monthly installment of Base Rent due for _____ is to be prorated as set out in the Lease. Thus, the Base Rent due for the _____ day period beginning _____ and ending on _____ is $_____. [IF APPLICABLE]

5. Each signer is fully authorized to execute this Memo.

    Please execute a signed counterpart of this Memo within _____ days of the date above. Please keep a signed copy for your records.

Faxed, PDF and electronic signatures are fully binding and may be used in place of original signatures.

Landlord's Signature: _____
Date: _____

AGREED TO AND ACCEPTED BY TENANT:

Tenant's Signature: _____
Date: _____

CALCULATION OF TOTAL COSTS OF OCCUPANCY

This form is designed to help a Tenant understand the total cost of occupancy of a particular space.

It aims to organize the details in a fairly easy to understand format. It can be used to get a general snapshot of costs for budgeting purposes, negotiating or comparison between prospects. For a more sophisticated economic measurement the user can discount future payment using a discount rate. In that case, the form should be modified as needed. This method will assist in comparing different deals. For example, a back-loaded transaction with lots of free rent late in the term may be compared on an apples to apples basis with a more straightforward transaction.

In addition to the form, we have attached an actual calculation of the Effective Rate per square foot using this method. Note that this is similar to the form which is attached to the rent comparison worksheet, but some may express a preference for one or the other.

Calculation of Total Costs of Occupancy Table

		Annual Base Rent	Annual Operating Costs	Utilities	Annual Parking	Other
A	Pre-Start Expenditures					
B	Credits & Incentives					
	Year 1					
	Year 2					
	Year 3					
	Year 4					
	Total					

Calculation Procedure:

1. Aggregate the totals of all components for the entire term to get grand total cost of occupancy. Place Pre-Start Expenditures and Credits & Incentives in the "Other" column.

2. Divide grand total by number of years to get effective rent per year.

    (Average)

3. Divide the average per year by the number of square feet.

4. The result is the annual effective rent per square foot.

Example of Average Annual Effective Rate Calculator

	Annual Base Rent	Annual Operating Costs	Utilities	Annual Parking	Other
Pre-Start Expenditures					$18,500
Credits & Incentives					($11,000)
Year 1	$20,000	$2,000	$1,900	$750	$750
Year 2	$20,400	$2,080	$1,976	$780	$750
Year 3	$20,808	$2,163	$2,055	$811	$750
Year 4	$21,224	$2,250	$2,137	$844	$750
Year 5	$21,649	$2,340	$2,223	$877	$750
Total	**$104,081**	**$10,833**	**$10,291**	**$4,062**	**$11,250**

This Assumes Five year Term
Base Rent increases at 2% per year
Other items are assumed to increase at 4% per year
Space leased is approximately 2,000 square feet

1. Grand total is $140,517

2. Average Annual Rent is $28,103

3. Average Effective Rent is $14.05

LEASE CHECKLIST

This checklist is rather generic and is put together so it can be used for most all of the common types of leases (retail, office, industrial or ground). It can help a Broker or its clients check off issues, review a lease, and identify items to be negotiated.

In order to help in the formulation of more personalized and specific forms, we have added thoughts and suggestions targeting specific forms for each kind of transaction so one can create individualized checklists for specific deals. These are identified as separate supplements - one for office, retail, industrial, and ground leases. They follow this form.

Please be aware that checklists are good, but in the end the parties will need to live with the deal. When you look at a lease, try to place yourself in the shoes of your client. Ask the following questions whenever you confront a provision or lease that seems out of the ordinary or when you sign off on a document:

a) Is the clause vague or ambiguous? If an educated person can't understand it then the drafter didn't do the job. Ask that it be cleared up.

b) Is a duty one-sided? Is one party held to a higher standard than the other? Normally most leases will be Landlord oriented, but sometimes a duty should be equally applied.

c) Are all relevant exhibits attached? Many times exhibits are the last things prepared and sometimes they are very important.

d) Have the economics been totally calculated? Is the tenant aware of the timing for payments? Example: Will tenant need to come up with the security deposit, the first month's rent and the last month's rent at time of execution even though tenant doesn't even get possession for six months? If the lease calls for annual 4% increases and the actual numbers are not spelled out, does the tenant realize that after 4 years, the original $5000 monthly rent will be $5,849 per month?

	Initial Draft	Major Issue	Final Draft
I. PARTIES/LEASED PREMISES			
A. Are Parties correctly identified?			
1. States of qualification?			
2. Names and addresses?			
B. Are Premises described in detail?			
1. Is the description clear and accurate?			
2. Is the square footage correct?			
3. Is an accurate floor plan attached?			
4. If options/expansion rights, are they shown?			
C. What is the method for determining the square footage?			
1. Does the Premises include usable SF only, or is there a common area factor added?			
2. Is the Load Factor clearly defined?			
D. Is there a right to measure space?			
1. Can Tenant's architect confirm?			
2. What is the timing for remeasurement?			
E. Is the Project described in detail?			
1. Is there an accurate site plan or survey attached?			
2. Is the description clear?			
3. Will future improvements be			

added?			
F. Are Common Areas well-defined?			
1. Can Landlord alter the Common Areas?			
2. Is there a nonexclusive right to use Common Areas?			
3. Is there provision regarding access or parking during Common Area construction?			
4. Is visibility protected?			
G. Is parking clearly defined?			
1. Is the number of spaces correct?			
2. Are there exclusive spaces?			
a. Need valet/drop-off area?			
b. Are handicap spaces appropriate for operation and sufficient in number?			
3. Are there any exclusions or restrictions?			
4. Does Landlord have a right to move parking spaces?			
5. What if parking decreases?			
II. TERM OF LEASE AND RENEWAL PROVISIONS			
A. Are the commencement and termination dates clear?			
1. When does rent commence?			
2. How are occupancy delays handled?			
a. Is there abatement?			

	b. Is the Lease term extended or is there a revision of the commencement date?			
	c. Will there be a "drop dead" date?			
	d. Tenant rights for free rent?			
	e. Tenant rights to terminate			
B. Are there Extension Options?				
	1. How many?			
	2. How long?			
C. What is the Extension Rate and Terms?				
	1. How is Rent determined?			
		a. Is there a minimum?		
		b. Is there a maximum?		
	2. Is Rent Fixed?			
		a. CPI? Other method?		
		b. If CPI, what is the standard?		
	3. If Rent is not fixed, what is the procedure?			
		a. Arbitration?		
		b. Who is arbitrator?		
		c. Baseball arbitration or other method?		
	4. Does the "Fair Market Rate" definition make sense?			
	5. Is Tenant entitled to any allowances/buildout at renewal?			
	6. Carpet Cleaning at renewal?			

	7.	Painting at renewal?			
	8.	Does Tenant have option to withdraw exercise of extension if arbitrated rent is not acceptable?			
D. Right to early possession?					

III. RENT PROVISIONS

A.	What is the format?				
	1.	Triple Net			
	2.	Gross			
	3.	Full Service with Base Year			
	4.	Other			
B.	Any Concessions				
	1.	Free Rent?			
	2.	Reduced Rent?			
C.	Rent Escalations				
	1.	When do increases take place?			
	2.	Are they fixed or by formula like CPI?			
	3.	Is there a cap on increases?			
D.	Shared Expenses				
	1.	What is Tenant's proportionate share?			
		a. How is share determined?			
		b. Is it fixed?			
		c. If this can change – how?			
	2.	Base Year for Operating			

	Expenses?			
E.	What is the definition of Operating Expenses?			
	1. Are appropriate exclusions in the Lease?			
	2. Is there a cap on controllables?			
	3. May Tenant audit operating expenses?			
	a. How long to audit?			
	b. If discrepancies, what are Tenant rights?			
F.	Are Operating Expenses estimated annually and paid monthly?			
G.	Percentage Rate applicable?			
	1. Are there appropriate definitions and exclusions?			
	2. When paid?			
	3. Is there a threshold for payment? What is the breakpoint?			
	4. Audit rights by Landlord?			
IV.	**SECURITY DEPOSIT**			
A.	Required?			
	1. Size of the deposit?			
	2. Is it Base Rent or Base plus additional?			
B.	Is it cash or note or letter of credit?			
C.	Is there a burn off or early release?			
D.	Is there a clear protocol on			

	transfer?			
E.	Able to apply against final month's rent?			

V. CONDITION OF THE PREMISES

A.	Is the Premises to be accepted in AS IS condition?			
B.	What warranties will be available?			
	1. Compliance with law?			
	2. Environmental?			
	3. Good working order?			
	4. Are certain systems warranted for periods of time (e.g. HVAC)?			
C.	Finished space or a shell? If finished, will it be a turn-key?			
D.	Does Lease clearly define the work to be carried out by Tenant? Landlord?			

VI. CONSTRUCTION PROVISIONS

A.	What are any build-out requirements?			
B.	Are Landlord obligations and Tenant obligations clear?			
C.	Are the timetables realistic?			
	1. Deliverables?			
	2. Approvals?			
D.	Landlord's work well defined?			
	1. Are there Tenant-approved plans and specifications?			
	2. Does Tenant have the right			

		to approve the budget?			
	3.	Does Tenant have the right to choose/approve contractors?			
	4.	Will the work be bid out?			
	5.	Can Tenant have early access to install fixtures, equipment, etc.?			
E.	Warranties regarding construction?				
F.	Is change order process appropriate?				
G.	Any construction management fees?				
	1.	What are they based on?			
	2.	Hard costs only?			
H.	Does Tenant have a right to approve budget?				
I.	In re: Tenant Buildout				
	1.	Are accurate building plans provided?			
	2.	Will Landlord approve the architect/contractor(s)?			
	3.	Is there any allowance?			
	4.	How is the allowance paid?			
	5.	Are change orders covered?			
J.	Punchlist process?				
	1.	When is a punchlist done?			
	2.	Time of completion?			
	3.	Method for enforcing?			

VII.	**USE BY TENANT**			
A.	What is the permitted use?			
	1. Does it accurately cover Tenant's needs/business?			
	2. Does the use include "any legal use?"			
	3. Is the use permitted by local law? Zoning? Will Landlord warrant?			
	4. Will Landlord represent that the use is legally permitted?			
	5. Are there explicit prohibited uses?			
B.	Are operating hours of the Building appropriate?			
VIII.	**LEGAL COMPLIANCE/WARRANTY**			
A.	Do the Premises and Project comply with applicable laws – including environmental zoning, grade, ADA, etc.?			
B.	Who pays for any work required to comply with law?			
C.	Is Landlord responsible for compliance prior to Lease commencement?			
IX.	**MAINTENANCE & REPAIR**			
A.	What are Tenant maintenance and repair obligations?			
B.	What are Landlord maintenance and repair obligations?			

	C.	Who owns improvements?			
	D.	Must Tenant provide service contracts?			
		1. HVAC?			
		2. Roof?			
		3. Other?			

X. OPERATING EXPENSES

	A.	What is the definition of Operating Costs?			
		1. Are provisions typical/appropriate?			
		2. Do fair exclusions apply?			
	B.	Is there a cap?			
	C.	Can the amount be increased each year?			

XI. UTILITIES

	A.	Who is responsible for utilities?			
	B.	Are utilities separately metered?			
	C.	If proration of utilities, how accomplished?			

XII. SERVICES

	A.	HVAC?			
		1. Is there a temperature range standard?			
		2. After hours? What are the costs?			
	B.	Security?			
		1. Who is responsible?			

	2.	What are standards?			
	3.	Any special key/access provisions?			
C.	Janitorial? Who is responsible?				

XIII. ALTERATIONS

A.	Can Tenant freely make non-structural changes?				
	1.	Is there a dollar amount above which approval is needed?			
	2.	Is there a construction administration fee?			
B.	If Landlord approval required, is it subject to reasonableness?				
C.	Are nonstructural alterations easily approved?				
D.	If alterations to be removed ad the end of the term, will Landlord provide removal notice at time of cause it consents to alterations?				
	1.	Can Tenant elect to leave alterations?			
	2.	Who owns the alterations?			
	3.	Who insures the alterations?			

XIV. LANDLORD ENTRY

A.	Does Landlord provide notice prior to entry?				
	1.	Is notice at least twenty-four (24) hours, except in emergency?			
	2.	Is entry limited to particular			

		purpose(s)?			
	B.	Is there a provision for no unreasonable interference with Tenant business?			
	C.	Are there special security issues in all parts of the Premises?			
		1. Should entry to certain areas be prohibited?			
	D.	May Landlord post signs on or show Premises?			

XV. TAXES

	A.	Is definition of taxes limited fairly to real estate taxes and assessment?			
	B.	Does Tenant pay the taxes?			
		1. Does Tenant have a right to file proceedings to contest/reduce?			
		2. Will Tenant receive its costs from tax savings?			
	C.	What is the method of prorating taxes at term beginning and ending?			
	D.	Does Tenant pay increase over base year?			
		1. If so, confirm the building fully assessed for tax purposes in the base year.			
	E.	Any protection from increases that are triggered by Landlord sale?			

XVI. INSURANCE

	A.	Have the insurance provisions been reviewed by insurance agent/risk manager?			

	B.	Are the Landlord's insurance obligations enough?		
	C.	Does Lease permit increase of the insurance limits by Landlord over time?		
	D.	Fire and casualty insurance – are Tenant needs met?		
	E.	Waiver of subrogation appropriate?		
	F.	Is blanket policy okay?		
	G.	Option to self-insure?		
XVII.	**INDEMNITY**			
	A.	Are Tenant's indemnity obligations limited to negligence?		
	B.	Is there indemnity for Landlord's negligence or breach?		
	C.	Is waiver of subrogation acceptable to insurance company?		
XVIII.	**DAMAGE AND DESTRUCTION**			
	A.	What is the time period for restoring?		
	B.	Who replaces Tenant's permanent alterations?		
	C.	Does Tenant have a right to terminate for major event? Casualty near end of term?		
	D.	Rent abatement?		
	E.	Are Landlord's repair obligations limited to insurance proceeds actually received?		
XIX.	**NON-DISTURBANCE**			
	A.	Is a Tenant given non-disturbance		

		agreement from lenders?			
	B.	Is SNDA attached?			
		1. Is it reasonable?			
		2. Does it change the Lease terms?			

XX.	**CONDEMNATION**				
	A.	What are the periods for restoration?			
	B.	Is there rent abatement if Tenant's business is interrupted?			
	C.	Is Rent equitably reduced?			
	D.	Does Tenant have rights of cancellation if taking substantially affects operation?			
	E.	Does Tenant share an award?			

XXI.	**ASSIGNMENT AND SUBLETTING**				
	A.	Can Landlord unreasonably withhold or delay consent?			
	B.	If Tenant assigns, is it released from liability?			
	C.	Are corporate transactions/sales/mergers exempt?			
	D.	Will Landlord share in sublease "profit?"			
	E.	Does Landlord charge for assignment/sublease reviews?			
	F.	Is there a Landlord recapture right?			

XXII.	**DEFAULT PROVISIONS**				
	A.	Is there adequate notice and opportunity to cure?			

	B.	What are the late fees?				
		1. When charged?				
		2. What is the penalty interest rate?				
	C.	Must Landlord mitigate damages?				
	D.	Is there acceleration of Rents?				
	E.	Does Landlord collect for amounts beyond Rent?				
	F.	Is there a Landlord default provision?				
		1. Can Tenant cure Landlord's default?				
		2. Set off rights?				
		3. Right for Tenant to terminate?				
XXIII.	**TENANT'S SURRENDER**					
	A.	Is return subject to reasonable wear and tear? Casualty? Landlord negligence?				
	B.	Must Tenant improvements/alterations be removed?				
		1. May Tenant leave cabling in place?				
		2. Need to remove permanent improvements?				
	C.	Is it clear that Tenant may remove its furniture, fixtures, and equipment?				
	D.	Any special requirements as to environmental?				

XXIV.	**HOLDOVER**			
	A.	What is the rental rate for holdover?		
	B.	Is there a limit on damages in case of holdover?		
XXV.	**TENANT SIGNAGE**			
	A.	Signage on exterior?		
	B.	If a monument sign, is Tenant listed?		
	C.	What are standards for signage? Who pays?		
	D.	If Tenant has a standard sign package, is that part of the Lease?		
	E.	Who removes at end of Lease?		
XXVI.	**ENVIRONMENTAL**			
	A.	Is Landlord responsible for pre-existing conditions?		
	B.	Does property have unique issues?		
	C.	Does Landlord bear cost regarding asbestos, underground tanks, etc.?		
	D.	Pre or post Lease audit?		
XXVII.	**LANDLORD LIABILITY**			
	A.	Is there a limited liability clause limited to equity?		
XXVIII.	**PURCHASE OPTION/RIGHT OF FIRST REFUSAL**			
	A.	Purchase Option?		
		1. Is price based on a formula or fixed?		

	2.	If appraisal based, what is formula?			
	3.	Will there be adjustments for Tenant expenditures?			
	4.	Time of exercise? Time for closing?			
	5.	Are the details of the sale like title, proration, etc., clearly stated?			
	B.	If ROFR, how long does it run?			
	1.	Time to elect?			
	2.	Are all terms spelled out?			
XXIX.	**GUARANTEES**				
	A.	Full? If limited – how?			
	B.	How long?			
	C.	If more than a single guarantor, are guaranties "several" or "joint and several"?			
XXX.	**BROKERAGE**				
	A.	Is it clear who pays?			
	B.	Is the deal accurately described?			
	C.	Names correct?			
XXXI.	**BOILERPLATE**				
	A.	Severability			
	B.	Governing Law/Judicial/Legal			
	1.	Does arbitration/mediation make sense?			
	2.	Is there a jury waiver?			
	3.	Will attorney fees be			

awarded?			
C. Estoppel Certificate			
D. Successors and Assigns			
E. No Waiver			
F. Lease Memorandum			
G. Captions			
H. Entire Agreement			
I. Counterparts			
J. Digital Execution			
K. Force Majeure			
L. Submission of Lease Non-binding			
M. Corporate Authority			
M. No Presumption against Draftees Party			
XXXII. EARLY TERMINATION/RIGHT TO REDUCE PREMISES			
A. How is it triggered?			
B. Is it one time or continuous?			
C. What are the payment obligations?			
1. If termination payments, are the calculations clear?			
2. When is payment due?			
XXXIII. RULES AND REGULATIONS			
A. Do the rules and regulations create operational issues?			
B. Do the rules and regulations modify the Lease			
C. Will rules be applied in fair/non-discriminating ways?			

	D.	Will Tenant get notice of rules changes?		

XXXIV. NOTICES

	A.	Are notices going to the correct place(s)?		
	B.	By stated delivery method?		
	C.	Who gets copies?		

XXXV. EXHIBITS

	A.	Are there any hidden terms or changes to the Lease?		
	B.	Are all attached?		

XXXVI. RELOCATION

	A.	Does Landlord have a right to relocate Tenant?		
	B.	Is Landlord required to act/consent reasonably?		
	C.	Limit on number of relocations?		
	D.	Costs covered?		

XXXVII. CONTINUOUS OPERATION

	A.	Are exceptions clearly stated?		
	B.	Co-Tenancy provisions?		

SUPPLEMENTS TO THE LEASING CHECKLIST

Office Supplement

1. Are parking issues thoroughly addressed – including exclusive spaces, monthly costs, etc.?
2. Determine if highway visibility or access issues are important. Are they dealt with?
3. Make sure that the signage requirements cover all needs.
4. Does the lease address sound-proofing?
5. Will the landlord pay for space planning?
6. Check to see if any need for 24/7 access is provided.
7. Pay attention to the delivery condition. Are both parties clear as to their responsibilities?
8. Expansion can be crucial. Is it addressed?
9. Study the documents to make sure utility costs and lighting cost provisions are thorough and understood.
10. Are security issues addressed appropriately? (Cameras, access etc.).
11. Are operating expenses thoroughly understood with caps and exclusions?
12. Will casualty clause present unworkable situation for tenant?
13. Will the rules and regulations affect the use and enjoyment by the particular tenant?
14. Are the "little things" addressed (i.e. bike rack, picnic areas, etc.)?

Retail Supplement

1. Pay special attention to the anchor tenant in a multi-tenant situation. Will that tenant continue to draw? Consider how long that Tenant will be staying and also think about co-tenancy provisions.
2. Tenants need to try hard to eliminate any relocation clause. Landlords need to determine if it is really necessary.
3. Make sure the parking accommodates needs.
4. Street visibility. Tenants don't want to be blocked from view. Landlords want flexibility to develop other properties.
5. Is there a stipulated square or will it be remeasured? At high costs per square foot this is particularly important.
6. Retail leases can generate areas for friction between the parties, - especially over audits, "neighbor issues", sound, smells, etc. Is the dispute resolved appropriately? Each party should see if the provision plays to its strengths and if it keeps costs down.
7. Is cost of ADA compliance addressed clearly? Who pays?
8. Do the lease provisions clearly address who will own the fixtures at the end of the lease term?
9. If there is a go-dark clause, tenant needs to think through all net results that can occur.
10. Are there particular E-Commerce issues that will arise? Pick up areas/need for extra loading areas/calculation or gross sales?
11. Thorough understanding of use restrictions and exclusions.
12. Trade name restrictions can be an issue for tenant and this cannot be glossed over.
13. Are there sufficient zoning permits, representations, and contingencies to assure the intended operation can go ahead?

Ground Lease Supplement

1. Condemnation issues are important. Who gets the proceeds in the case of a taking?
2. Lease subordination terms are central. The landlord will usually not want to subordinate its' interest and will want to make sure there are limits on the types of loans, the kind of lender and the notification of defaults. The tenant lender is making a significant investment and wants to be protected – especially if subordinated.
3. Pay attention to tax provision. Is there any tax on execution? If real estate taxes are in arrears, does the tax survive closing? Can Tenant appeal taxes?
4. Casualty issues need to be dealt with. If a casualty occurs near the end of the term, must tenant rebuild? Who holds proceeds of insurance? Who actually rebuilds?
5. Is the use broad enough given the long term?
6. Can the leasehold lender cure defaults?
7. Are the rent provisions sufficiently sensitive to the length and nature of the lease?
8. Be particularly careful of environmental uses and allocation of responsibility.
9. Will the tenant's lender be able to know of renewals, cure defects, and always protect its interests?
10. Are construction standards adequately addressed - ranging from budget to design, plans, specifications and construction? Want to anticipate issues and reduce friction during the construction phase.
11. Are the assignment and sublease provisions workable for the tenant and tenant's lender?
12. What happens to the improvements at the end of term?

Industrial Supplement

1. Do the surfaces in the space/lot accommodate the tenant's fork lift needs?
2. Make sure the Lease addresses needs like yard space, turning radius, scales, etc.
3. What kind of power does the tenant need? Will the power needs be appropriately addressed?
4. Stress the current state and future need, for sprinkler and its relocation to stacking height and other tenant operational issues.
5. Does yard space need to be fenced? Is this covered?
6. Utilities are vital. Make sure costs and quantity/quality are thoroughly addressed.
7. Are expansion needs addressed?
8. Is mezzanine space an issue? Who imposes it? What is cost?
9. Will zoning be a problem? Will hours of dock use etc. be controlled?
10. Environmental issues can be vital. Who cleans up problems of contaminants on the site?
11. Are docks and dock doors adequately addressed?
12. Can the space be modified easily for other uses to accommodate subletting?
13. Are security needs adequately addressed?
14. Is rail involved/addressed?

SECTION V: TECHNOLOGY AND MARKETING/PROFESSIONAL RESOURCES

"Any sufficiently advanced technology is indistinguishable from magic."

~ Arthur C. Clarke

INTRODUCTION

The commercial real estate Broker has the ability to benefit from an awesome array of technological tools and marketing/professional resources. Many of the tasks described in this book can be better performed with technology or outside assistance. In essence, these tools can serve to relieve the Broker of non-essential tasks, speed processes and research and avoid mistakes and inefficiencies. They do not replace the skills that elevate a commercial Broker: the human skills necessary to advise a client as to the best way to fulfill its needs and attain its goals.

Here are some technologies/programs/resources available to commercial Brokers. Our descriptions are just thumbnail sketches. We recommend visiting the various websites and seeing the fantastic array of powerful engines available to drive your business forward.

A lot of the resources below can fit within several different categories, so rather than breaking them up, we have compiled for you a list of resources including listing platform services, research property data, marketing services and more:

- **42Floors** is a comprehensive national search engine stocked with images, flyers, and floor plans for investors. It includes a separate lease section and provides information on available space. www.42floors.com

- **Boundless Network** is a branded goods marketing firm which helps Brokers build a brand that stands out from the crowd. www.boundlessnetwork.com

- **Buildout** is a targeted marketing array for Brokers which features instant document creation, branded email marketing, interactive site plans, property websites and more. www.buildout.com

- **Catylist** provides commercial lease information in 45+ markets. It includes analytics, customized reporting, listing search and more. It aims to give national exposure to its members. www.catylist.com

- **ChainXY** provides a data solutions with chain list data for retail, restaurant and real estate professionals. Quality business location information can drive the tenant site selection process. www.chainxy.com

- **CIMLS** is a leading free commercial property listing service. You can research and list properties for lease. www.cimls.com

- **ClientLook** is an all-in-one CRM built specifically for the commercial real estate industry. www.clientlook.com

- **CommissionTrac** was built to get commercial real estate agents paid faster and to streamline brokerage back office operations with accounting automation and organizational transparency. **www.commissiontrac.com**

- **CompStak** provides analyst reviewed comps, including timely leasing comps on a nationwide basis. **www.compstak.com**

- **CoStar** is a super powerful source of substantial research and reliable information on a vast number of commercial real estate properties. It gives the Broker tools to help get deals done. **www.costar.com**

- **CREXi** is a platform featuring a large number of property listings enabling the Broker to list and to find listings and close deals faster. **www.crexi.com**

- **Dealsumm** offers abstraction of leases and other real estate documents made easy. **www.dealsumm.com**

- **Digsy Al** is a commercial real estate CRM with a number of tools including built-in call display, mass email, templates, property tracking, and data-entry & workflow automation. **www.digsy.ai**

- **DocuSign** provides electronic signature technology and digital transaction management services. By facilitating electronic exchanges of contracts and signed documents, you can get deals done faster. **www.docusign.com**

- **Griddig** is a mobile and PC office leasing app. It includes tools aimed at speeding and smoothing the office space leasing process. **www.griddig.com**

- **Helium SEO** Experts at SEO strategies, they help Brokers cultivate better leads and build business. They are effective at promoting top position for local business searches – a major need for most brokerage firms. **www.helium-seo.com**

- **ID Plans** documents space and plans using cutting-edge cloud-based technology. They quickly give the space a profile that help speed up the leasing process. **www.idplans.com**

- **InCloud Counsel** is a leading expertise source for lease abstracts, confidentiality agreements, etc. They provide a cloud-based platform that can reduce legal costs and speed processes. **www.incloudcounsel.com**

- **Intalytics** furnishes intelligent real estate analytics for location selection. They help provide important insight depending on the industry. **www.intalytics.com**

- **LoopNet** is a premier commercial real estate marketing platform for commercial real estate professionals to reach over 5 million end users. **www.loopnet.com**

- **PropertySend** is commercial real estate marketing platform offering digital email marketing to a database of 120k+ contacts. **www.propertysend.com**

- **RealDash** is a platform with integrated tools to help automate the deal process and eliminate the need to work with multiple programs. It is customizable and let you create brochures, design websites, send email campaigns, track leads, etc. **www.realdash.com**

- **Retail Lease Trac** is a source for lease generation in the retail industry. They have demographic information, expansion plans, contact information, etc. **www.rltrac.com**

- **RealMassive** is a commercial real estate marketplace and data provider. It enables the industry to list and discover over 6 billion square feet of office, retail, and industrial space, and includes solutions for listing and tenant Brokers. **www.realmassive.com**

- **RealNex** is a comprehensive suite of tools for commercial real estate brokerage professionals. It includes comparative lease analysis, a marketing center, a powerful tenant rep and leasing agent app, and more. www.realnex.com

- **Relocation Strategies** has expertise coordinating and managing corporate and facility moves. By expertly handling the move management, they can cut down time and costs reducing relocation allowances, unnecessary rent loss, etc. www.relocationstrategies.net

- **Reonomy** is a large CRE data platform with coverage of over 47 million commercial properties. You can filter the data in various ways to get what you need first. **www.reonomy.com**

- **2-D As-Built Floor Plans** provides cutting edge technology to measure square footage accurately. www.2dfloorplans.com

- **TheAnalyst PRO** is a fast, powerful commercial real estate analysis platform. It helps with comprehensive lease analysis of leases vs. your own analysis, among other things. www.theanalystpro.com

- **theBrokerList (tBL)** is an interactive directory for the commercial real estate industry. **www.thebrokerlist.com**

- **The Content Funnel** creates Content Marketing plans exclusively for real estate companies and professionals. They can help with writing your blog, building your brand, etc. www.thecontentfunnel.com

- **The News Funnel** is a content platform for the commercial real estate industry. You can receive real estate news curated for you based on your news. **www.thenewsfunnel.com**

- **TourIt Media, Inc** is one of the top video, 3D and virtual reality companies dedicated to the commercial real estate field. They can quickly build world-class content to make space visualization easier. **www.touritmedia.com**

- **Yardi Matrix** offers comprehensive commercial real estate intelligence. You can obtain deep property information including detailed lease comps. **www.yardimatrix.com**

SECTION VI: LEARNING THROUGH EXPERIENCE

"Wealth is the ability to fully experience life."

~ Henry David Thoreau

INTRODUCTION

We have had the enormous privilege of dealing with some outstanding real estate professionals in our career. It is individuals like those introduced here who make the business extra special. We asked some folks to provide us with anecdotes from their lives in the business – especially leasing situations.

Tip:

Connect. The ability to network online is fantastic, but a wealth of new listings and new knowledge is available to the persistent Broker who meets folks face to face. Bankers, friends of friends, cocktail party acquaintances, love to talk real estate. Listen, learn and use your social skills to build your business.

These two anecdotes are from Dave Noonan, a respected industrial broker in the greater Cincinnati area:

Anecdote 1

About 10 years ago, a well-known Cincinnati tenant rep retail broker who represented a national chain was asked to negotiate a lease renewal on behalf of the company. The lease was in an excellent Cincinnati area in a small, locally-owned strip center, relatively new, and one of the adjoining tenants had gone dark due to business conditions. The company, thinking it would be a good time to negotiate a renewal at perhaps a better lease rate, asked the broker to see what he could do. The broker did not know the building owner, so made assumptions that the owner would be nervous and wanting to tie down an existing tenant. Bad decision.

About 4 months prior to the lease expiration, the broker contacted the building owner, introduced himself as the exclusive representative of the tenant, and said that the tenant would like to negotiate a long-term renewal, but that the first year of the renewal would have a lease rate 20% below the present rate. The owner seemed interested, asked a few questions, said he understood, and the conversation ended. The broker waited a few weeks, not wanting to appear anxious, and after about a month contacted the owner again, expressing mild surprise that he had not heard anything. The owner politely informed him that he appreciated his efforts, but that he was not interested in the deal that was presented. The broker then apologized for the misunderstanding, and said that his suggested proposal was only a starting point. The owner said that he understood. The broker then suggested that it was entirely possible that by the time their negotiations were finished, that the lease rate might be closer to the existing rate than what was previously mentioned. The owner said he appreciated the clarification, said that he now understood more of the company's intentions, and would think about it.

A month went by and the broker was unsuccessful in getting ahold of the owner, as both were traveling and missed several of each other's calls. With 6 or 7 weeks left on the lease term, the broker again called the owner and said that his client would like to have a lease extension prepared at the current lease rate or maybe slightly more rent per month. The owner said he understood, and said he'd begin working on it. When several more weeks went by, the broker was getting nervous, and when he finally reached the owner, asked where the extension document was. The owner said that he was preparing it but had stopped as he wasn't comfortable with the lease rate the broker had suggested. At this point the broker was quite agitated, and asked the owner to prepare the extension with the lease rate that he wanted.

Several more weeks went by, and the broker again called the owner who said he was close to producing a document. A week later an extension document was sent to the broker with many of the lease terms changed and with a 50% increase in rent. The broker expressed outrage, and said that he doubted that his client would agree to most of the changes. He reminded the Owner - not smart - that they were in the midst of a market downturn.

More time went by, and within the last weeks of the original term, the broker produced a response to the document and a short-term extension agreement as well. When he reached the owner, and had delivered the documents, the owner said that he would not sign a short-term extension. He also said that he wanted to read and digest the suggested changes to the extension agreement. The broker made him promise that they could talk in the next few business days, and within a week, they did. The owner then said that he was not going to agree to the changes proposed. The broker then asked if anyone else was ready to lease the space, and the owner said no, and that his client could tell him that nobody had toured the space.

Within hours, the broker and his client got on the phone with the owner. They said that they were willing to agree to the document as proposed by the owner with the 50% increase. Their only copy had been marked up and they had no other. The owner, at this point said that he would not sign an extension at all. He said that if the tenant had contacted him directly, or even with the broker, and had simply asked for an extension proposal, he would have produced one, most likely with no real major changes and with some slight rent increases. But he said at this point, he was finished with the process. The tenant had a very large holdover rent provision in the original lease, and had to pay it, and also discharged their tenant rep broker. The owner was a well-to-do local investor who was less interested in the money and more interested in a smooth process.

The broker should have known this, or should have figured this out early on.

Anecdote 2

A rookie broker - let's call him Jim - was working for one of the larger companies attempting to get some traction in industrial brokerage. Inevitably he'd end up calling a client that had done business with one of his teammates. If it was recent, he'd just go on to the next one.

But one day he called a guy whose last contact with a teammate was 5 years earlier. Let's say this teammate's name was Bob. Thinking this may mean that the time elapsed made the contact fair game, he consulted a senior broker, and asked his advice. It went something like this:

J (for Jim) "So Bob told me he hadn't talked to XXX in over 5 years. What should I do?"

SB (Senior Broker) "Go to Bob and tell him"

J "But what if he tells me to leave the guy alone?"

SB "Look, he'll do one of 3 things. He'll tell you to go ahead and pursue it, he'll tell you that you and he can work on it together, or he'll tell you to bug off, that he'll handle it"

J "Well what if he does the last thing?"

SB "So, then you tell him that you don't think that's fair, and walk away"

J "How about if it happens again?"

SB "Then you say to him, you know, Bob, there's a pattern here, I'm turning up leads that you've let slide, and you're taking advantage, and leaving me with nothing"

J "Well, then, what?"

SB "If Bob is reasonable, he'll cave in, and at the very least share the deal with you. If he's a jackass, he'll do the same thing"

J "So what's your point?"

SB "How much is the potential commission?"

J "I don't know, maybe 10 grand"

SB " So the point is, if Bob's a jackass, nobody cares what he thinks, but if he's not, do you think $10 grand is enough to erase the stain of a broker going around the market saying YOU are a jackass??

This is from John Clark, a major Broker in Syracuse, New York.

Everyone enjoys discussing commercial real estate. In my younger, cold calling days, I'd stop in to call on tenants and, many times, the executive in the corner office would come out to ask me "What's going on in the area?" They wanted the latest scoop on anything new in the market. They may not have had a real estate need that day, but they would someday. And I met them face to face.

Make sure people know what you do. You'll be surprised at how often they'll ask the same thing those executives did. You not only get to show your market knowledge, but make a connection that they'll often remember.

This anecdote comes from an experienced west coast real estate pro.

Broker had put together a very lucrative 10-year lease deal for his landlord client. When they were about to sign the lease, the landlord balked, claiming the commission was too high. He asked the Broker to reduce his commission. The Broker declined to give into this heavy-handed tactic – after all, he had already agreed to the landlord's demand to no commission except during the Prime Term.

Well the landlord thought he was really smart. He approached the tenant and offered a 5-year term with a 5-year renewal at the original rent. The tenant was happy to oblige since this way it would have the same deal with less long-term liability.

Year 5 came. Guess what? The tenant declined to renew. Landlord's greed cut his own throat. Naturally, the Broker had a very hollow revenge since he only made half of what he earned, but at least he got to see the old adage get played out – "Pigs get fat. Hogs get slaughtered."

This is from David Ballard, who is an experienced developer as well as commercial real estate broker.

(Note: Mr. Ballard has handled a wide range of transactions and done it all. His contribution here provides insight into the special rewards that a career in commercial real estate can provide. It is not just about the money. Remember this when you start to get caught up in the mere dollars and cents.)

Over the last few decades I have had the privilege of working on affordable housing projects in El Paso, Texas. A border town of approximately 650,000 people and adjacent to its "Sister City", Juarez Mexico. While the border certainly presents significant cultural and economic challengers there are few greater challenges than providing affordable housing opportunities to first generation families that have come to America legally and in search of a better life.

Through various governmental programs such as USDA Rural Development we have provided well over 2500 deserving families with safe, sanitary affordable housing options. While the program is cumbersome for the builder the rewards of seeing families secure a real home in the United States is, at times, overwhelming.

One of the most rewarding programs we worked on was a collaboration with the Texas Department of Housing and Community Affairs, the Texas Work Force Commission and Socorro Independent School District. The effort entailed the construction of ten (10) homes and having High School students, enrolled in shop classes building tables and bird houses, to get real world experience in building homes. The effort was also aimed at providing an understanding to a small generation of students the meaning of affordability and sustainability.

The homes were basic in design but included south facing orientations, window sizing and placement to increase solar gain in the winter and reduce it in the summer. Floor coverings that would warm in the winter sun light and stay cool in the summer heat. Walls constructed with 2x6s to support increased insulation and heavier insulation in the ceilings. To save on construction costs the homes were completed to a point that they were certainly livable yet leaving portions unfinished allowing the new home owners to have the smallest possible house payment and finish items in the home as time and finances allowed.

Once the project was completed we all received accolades from the State of Texas, the Workforce Commission and school district. But what was most meaningful to me occurred about one year later while I was on another job site.

A young man saw and recognized me from about 100 yards away and began running towards me yelling my name. I was certainly confused as to what was going on but soon learned that he had been one of the young men at the high school who participated in the program. When he reached me, out of breath and smiling from ear to ear, he grabbed my hand and shook it vigorously, thanking me profusely for the opportunity to participate in the program because it led to a job for him with a local home builder. He explained that he had placed the experience on his resume and it intrigued his employer who wanted to find out more. It led to an opportunity for this young man that he felt he would not have had without the experience he had gained through this program.

I must admit that I was speechless and even a bit choked up at the whole experience. But this young man gave me the best reward and gift I could have ever received, and it will stay with me the rest of my life. The difference you make in even one life can truly change the future of a generation. I was and am humbled and sincerely, grateful for the experience.

This anecdote comes from Si Pitstick, a very successful Broker in the Cincinnati Area.

I was doing a showing at an industrial location. It was dark and I wasn't able to see the floor very well. It turns out I had stepped squarely on a sticky surface rat trap. Not only did the rat trap affix itself to my shoe, but when I tried to remove it things just got worse. I went outside to the gravel lot to try and get the thing off. The gravel started to affix to my shoe, the trap, and my trousers. The moral of the story is, of course "in commercial real estate watch your step."

This comes from Larry Bergman, one of the authors.

I probably should title this by the same name as Steve Martin's funny movie—"The Jerk." It happened recently and involves a lease on a new property purchased by a great guy who our firm is proud to represent. A new tenant, claiming financial difficulties approached the landlord and asked for a huge rent reduction—say more than 50% of the rent. My client consulted his lawyer and also asked me for advice. I felt, under the circumstances—fresh lease, market rate, lots of term, good property location, etc.—that chasing the rent down was not the way to go. My idea in this kind of scenario is to tell the tenant that you will assist in helping locate a sublessee or maybe even an assignee, but that there is no good reason to take an immediate haircut. Naturally, you would want to work with them to give them a short-term reduction—a reduction with a note to be paid later, etc.—but accepting a huge hit with no potential better result doesn't make sense to me. If you do any accommodating for a tenant in this situation, you want to be sure that there is lease language that keeps them from subletting and keeping the sublease profit. Otherwise you look bad.

The lawyer for the client, who I never dealt with and is unknown to me, was all for the haircut. He counseled for the low rent and his argument prevailed with the landlord. Naturally it's the client's decision, which is the way to go, but when the landlord requested that I speak with this lawyer, the attorney was rude, condescending and heavy handed. "The Jerk". There was room to disagree, and I get that, but there is never any reason to be disrespectful or unprofessional—ESPECIALLY WHEN WE ARE ON THE SAME SIDE.

Naturally what I think happened is the lawyer felt I was second guessing him. That was not my intent. I suspect he is sensitive and doesn't have a lot of self-confidence, or perhaps experience, and was afraid of looking bad to his client. I never did that in any way and in our dealings I kept my cool and believe I was polite and professional.

The moral of this one I think is three-fold: a) don't accept the long-term one-way haircut as the only way to solve a problem with a weak tenant; b) treat others like you want to be treated; and c) try to hold your tongue and keep from saying something you'll regret even when you're dealing with someone who is very unprofessional.

A special thanks goes to the following:

David Ballard
Jeff Beals
Kathy Bergman
Steve Bove
Emilee Buttrum
John Clark
Jessica Drake
Rachel Ely
Paul Gallenstein
Michael Green
Max Hopkins
Ed Neyra
Dave Noonan
Si Pitstick
Josh Robinson
Cierra Sanders
William Schottenstein
Laura Spears
Jessica Tepe, Esq.
Gary Webb, Esq.

www.ingramcontent.com/pod-product-compliance
Lightning Source LLC
Chambersburg PA
CBHW071530220526
45469CB00003B/716